DR. NO

DR. NO

The First James Bond Film

JAMES CHAPMAN

Wallflower Press
New York

Wallflower Press is an imprint of Columbia University Press
Columbia University Press
Publishers Since 1893
New York   Chichester, West Sussex
cup.columbia.edu
Copyright © 2022 James Chapman
All rights reserved

Library of Congress Cataloging-in-Publication Data

Names: Chapman, James, 1968– author.
Title: Dr. No : the first James Bond film / James Chapman.
Description: New York : Wallflower Press, [2022] | Includes bibliographical references and index.
Identifiers: LCCN 2022011477 (print) | LCCN 2022011478 (ebook) | ISBN 9780231204927 (hardback) | ISBN 9780231204934 (trade paperback) | ISBN 9780231555746 (ebook)
Subjects: LCSH: Dr. No (Motion picture) | James Bond films—History and criticism.
Classification: LCC PN1997.D7247 C48 2022 (print) | LCC PN1997.D7247 (ebook) | DDC 791.43/72—dc23/eng/20220604
LC record available at https://lccn.loc.gov/2022011477
LC ebook record available at https://lccn.loc.gov/2022011478

Cover design: Elliott S. Cairns
Cover image: Collection Christophel / Alamy Stock Photo

For Nick Cull

CONTENTS

Acknowledgments ix

Introduction 1

1 Sex, Snobbery, and Sadism 13

2 Everything or Nothing 39

3 Monkey Business 65

4 Underneath the Mango Tree 91

5 A Bizarre Comedy Melodrama 123

6 I'm Just Looking 151

Conclusion 183

Appendix I: Dr. No *Production Credits* 187
Appendix II: Dr. No *Production Budget* 191
Appendix III: Dr. No *Daily Progress Reports* 195
Notes 203
Bibliography 225
Index 233

ACKNOWLEDGMENTS

THE IDEA for a stand-alone book on the first James Bond film occurred to me after *Dr. No* was screened at Cinema Ritrovato XXXIII in Bologna, Italy in June 2019, as part of a strand of Technicolor Archive prints. The fact that the "expert" introduction to the film focused largely on David Lean and *Lawrence of Arabia* rather than *Dr. No* brought home to me the extent to which the Bond films are still not always recognized as belonging to the accepted "canon" of film history. With October 2022 marking the sixtieth anniversary of the release of *Dr. No* in the United Kingdom, this seems the right moment to take a fresh look at the movie that launched the longest-running continuous film series in the history of motion pictures.

Another reason for returning to *Dr. No* is the availability of archival sources that were not available when I first wrote about this subject in *Licence to Thrill: A Cultural History of the James Bond Films* (1999) and which have shed significant new light on

ACKNOWLEDGMENTS

the production contexts of the film. The Film Finances Archive—the company that provided the guarantee of completion for *Dr. No*—includes a wide range of primary sources, including the financing and distribution agreements, budgets, cost reports, progress reports, and miscellaneous production correspondence. My thanks to James Shirras, David Korda, and Thoko Malvene at the London office of Film Finances for their exceptional generosity in supporting my research. I am also indebted to Mary Huelsbeck and the Wisconsin Historical Society at the University of Wisconsin–Madison for providing copies of materials from the United Artists Collection held by the Wisconsin Center for Film and Theater Research, and to Lindsay Moen and the University of Iowa Special Collections for materials from the Richard Maibaum papers.

I should like to record my thanks to Eon Productions for allowing access to the digitized treatments and scripts of *Dr. No* from the Richard Maibaum papers.

I am happy to acknowledge the example of fellow Bond and film scholars whose work has informed this study: Llewella Chapman, Klaus Dodds, Sheldon Hall, Claire Hines, Tobias Hochscherf, and Andrew Spicer. Bond collectors and enthusiasts Gary J. Firuta and Peter Lorenz have generously provided materials from their own collections. And my colleagues in the School of Arts at the University of Leicester have, as ever, offered valuable intellectual support, even when the Great Coronavirus Lockdown of 2020–2021 meant that those "corridor conversations" went online.

My thanks to Ryan Groendyk and the team at Columbia University Press for their enthusiastic response to my suggestion

ACKNOWLEDGMENTS

of a stand-alone book on *Dr. No* and to the readers for their exceptionally supportive comments and feedback on the proposal.

I am fortunate that my wife, Llewella, is also a Bond aficionado, and understands the peculiar obsessions of the academic researcher. By happy coincidence, we have been working on our separate Bond projects in parallel and have been able to share research findings and exchange drafts throughout—and to share those "Eureka" moments, such as the time when I read the first script treatment and declared: "Dr. No was *never* a monkey!"

It is a pleasure to dedicate this book to Nicholas J. Cull, professor of public diplomacy at the University of Southern California—an excellent scholar, a trusted collaborator, and, above all, a much valued friend.

DR. NO

INTRODUCTION

WHEN DR. NO opened at the London Pavilion cinema on October 5, 1962, no one could have predicted that James Bond would still be going strong some twenty-five films and sixty years later. Most contemporary accounts suggest that producers Harry Saltzman and Albert R. "Cubby" Broccoli and distributor United Artists were thinking of a series of six films (at most) based on the popular spy novels of Ian Fleming before they ran out of economic and cultural energy. By 1975, when it was first shown on television in the United Kingdom, *Dr. No* had returned total worldwide theatrical rentals (the amount returned to the distributor after exhibitors have taken their share of the box office) of US$22.1 million, which, even allowing for the fact that some of that total came from numerous reissues, nevertheless represented a very significant profit for a film that cost a little over $1 million to make.[1] Its success was surpassed by the films that followed. By 1966, the first four Bond films—*Dr. No*

INTRODUCTION

was followed by *From Russia with Love* (1963), *Goldfinger* (1964), and *Thunderball* (1965)—had earned total rentals of over $100 million.[2] *Dr. No* was the origin of what became the longest-running continuous series in film history. The Bond pictures span half the entire history of cinema—a remarkable production achievement regardless of what one thinks about the quality of the films themselves.

If *Dr. No* now seems a relatively modest affair in comparison to some of the films that followed—one thinks here of the expensive production values, massive sets and epic spectacle of later Bond pictures such as *You Only Live Twice* (1967), *The Spy Who Loved Me* (1977), and *Moonraker* (1979)—it nevertheless set the template for the rest of the series: outlandish plots, improbable heroism, colorful locations, bizarre villains, beautiful women, spectacular action set pieces, and a distinctive style of parodic tongue-in-cheek humor. It is difficult today to appreciate just how different from the usual cinema fare *Dr. No* must have seemed to audiences in the early 1960s. Anecdotal evidence of its impact on cinema-goers in Britain is provided by future James Bond star Timothy Dalton: "The first Bond movie I saw was *Dr. No*, in my local cinema in a place called Belper in Derbyshire. I must have been about thirteen or fourteen years old . . . The only movies we'd seen were war pictures, or drawing room comedies, or westerns, and here was something right up to date and really terrific."[3]

My aim in writing this short monograph is to relocate the film within its original historical and cultural contexts. Much of the critical and historical literature on the Bond films—including my own previous excursion into the field in *Licence*

INTRODUCTION

to Thrill: A Cultural History of the James Bond Films (1999)—
has focused on the Bond pictures as a series or franchise: scholars have focused on mapping the films' changing representations of geopolitics, national identity, and gender in response to wider shifts in British (and Western) society at large, and to analyzing the development or evolution of the Bond formula as an industrial and cultural mode of genre filmmaking. The emphasis has been on how they have adapted to changes in film culture and have functioned as a barometer of a shifting political and social landscape. *Dr. No* clearly holds an important place in the history of celluloid Bond, but it tends to be seen in relation to the films that followed: as the prototype for the series, "the first James Bond film." However, *Dr. No* did not spring from nowhere: its production—and success—were the outcome of historically specific industrial, economic, and cultural contexts.

It seems to me that if there is one Bond film that deserves a stand-alone volume, it is *Dr. No*. For one thing, the charge so often levelled against the Bond films by unsympathetic critics—that they are formulaic and repetitive, the very essence of filmmaking by numbers—cannot be made against this first picture for the simple reason that there was no Bond formula at the time. Indeed, the reception discourses of *Dr. No*, especially as exemplified by the film trade press, suggest that it sat outside standard genre categories. The British trade paper *Kine Weekly*, for example, described it not as a spy film or action picture, but as "a bizarre comedy melodrama."[4]

The consensus among film scholars and Bond aficionados is that *Dr. No* was something of a "sleeper" (an unexpected

INTRODUCTION

commercial success). Alexander Walker, for example, contends that "not a single person had the slightest inkling of the phenomenon they were launching" and "there was no belief that anything but a routine 'actioner' would emerge."[5] Roy Armes similarly suggests that "even when it was complete no one seems to have realized quite the dimensions of the success in store. In retrospect it is clear that Saltzman and Broccoli were right in all the crucial decisions, most important of which was the casting of Sean Connery [figure 0.1] as Bond."[6] Indeed, a narrative persists that United Artists thought it had backed a pig in a poke with *Dr. No*: it is widely reported that one executive commented following a preview screening that "the only good thing about the picture is that we can only lose a million dollars."[7] And Cubby Broccoli claimed that even after it had been

FIGURE 0.1 "Saltzman and Broccoli were right in all the crucial decisions, most important of which was the casting of Sean Connery as Bond." *Dr. No* (Danjaq LLC/United Artists Corporation, 1962).

INTRODUCTION

released to great popular acclaim in Britain and Europe, United Artists was reluctant to get behind it in the United States: "Several of the UA bookers who saw the picture privately in our projection room expressed the doubt that they could sell a picture in the major US cities with 'a Limey truck driver in the lead.'"[8] However, as this book will demonstrate, there is good reason to doubt this narrative even though it was propagated by the Bond producers themselves. Other sources suggest that United Artists was fully behind the film and that, far from being a sleeper, the success of *Dr. No* was due to the choice of a highly commercial property and an effective promotional strategy.

Dr. No broke the mold of popular cinema in several respects. Before it, there had been very few spy thrillers that could be considered genuine "A" features: Alfred Hitchcock's *North by Northwest* (1959) and John Frankenheimer's *The Manchurian Candidate* (1962)—the latter released shortly after *Dr. No*—were exceptions in a genre that otherwise consisted largely of "B" movies. Most previous thriller or detective series, such as Bulldog Drummond, Dick Tracy, The Saint, and The Falcon, had tended to be supporting features for the lower half of a double bill. Terence Young, the director of *Dr. No*, remarked in one interview that Fleming's books were the sort of material previously associated with the studios of Hollywood's "Poverty Row": "Well, when you analyse it, and this is no disrespect to Ian, they were very sophisticated 'B'-picture plots. If someone tells you, 'A James Bond film,' you'd say, 'My God, that's for Monogram,' or Republic Pictures, who used to be around in those days. You would never have thought of it as a serious 'A' film."[9]

INTRODUCTION

To this extent, *Dr. No* may be placed within a broader trend in the film industry in the 1950s and 1960s. This is the process that film historians Kristin Thompson and David Bordwell have described as the "upscaling of genre": the production of what had hitherto been B-picture material with the budgets and production values of A-class features. This process can be seen, for instance, in the emergence of the high-end western in the late 1950s, exemplified by films such as *Gunfight at the O.K. Corral* (1957), *The Big Country* (1958), and *The Magnificent Seven* (1960), and in the first science-fiction blockbusters, *2001: A Space Odyssey* (1968) and *Planet of the Apes* (1968), at the end of the 1960s. Later leading exponents of genre upscaling were "movie brats" George Lucas and Steven Spielberg, who remade the space opera and adventure serials of their youth into the box-office blockbusters *Star Wars* (1977) and *Raiders of the Lost Ark* (1981). However, nowhere was the process more apparent than in the emergence of the contemporary action thriller as a major production trend:

> The effect of amplifying B-film material was perhaps most visible in the rise of the big-budget espionage film. Hitchcock's elegant *North by Northwest* (1959) featured an innocent bystander caught up in a spy ring, but the catalyst for genre upscaling was Ian Fleming's fictional British agent James Bond. After two screen adaptations of the novels, 007 became a proven commodity with the phenomenally profitable *Goldfinger* (1964).[10]

Goldfinger was the film that made the commercial breakthrough for the Bond series in the US market (though, as we shall see, the idea that *Dr. No* was not successful there stands in need of correction). In Britain, the early Bond films exemplified a trend toward bigger films that eclipsed more routine fare at the box office. As Bill Altria, editor of *Kine Weekly*, observed in 1963: "The really big pictures—big at the box-office that is—are attracting larger audiences and more money in cinemas than ever before, but the run-of-the-mill films, the type that only a year ago were the bread and butter of the business, are barely yielding a crust."[11]

Dr. No also exemplified the changing production ecology of the film industry in the early 1960s. It was a case of what was known as a "runaway" production: the strategy whereby Hollywood companies invested in overseas production in order to benefit from lower costs and local subsidies while at the same time providing a level of production values that would allow the films to be released in America on a level playing field with domestic features. To this extent, *Dr. No* may be located within a trend that also included films such as *The African Queen* (1951), *The Bridge on the River Kwai* (1957), *The Guns of Navarone* (1961), *Lawrence of Arabia* (1962), and *Zulu* (1964). It exemplified an Anglo-American production ecology: a combination of US dollars (United Artists) and British cultural capital (Ian Fleming's novel). The production base at Pinewood Studios and the employment of largely British crews meant that the Bond films met the statutory requirements for registration as British films; however, the production values and foreign locations positioned them as "international" pictures at a time when many British films were parochial comedies or war films produced essentially for domestic consumption. The reception discourses of *Dr. No*

INTRODUCTION

positioned it squarely as a British film, but it was a different sort of British film than critics and audiences were used to: it was not a social realist drama or an adaptation of a prestigious literary property, but an unashamedly popular genre film in a tradition of sensational "thick-ear" melodrama.

Until now, the most thoroughgoing account of the making of *Dr. No* was the special issue of *Cinema Retro* published to coincide with the film's fiftieth anniversary in 2012.[12] This includes a wealth of anecdotal material compiled from interviews over many years with members of the cast and crew. The problems of relying on interviews in researching film history are well known, of course: memory can be unreliable after so many years and sometimes there is a tendency to reinterpret events with the benefit of hindsight or to recycle well-known anecdotes of dubious origin. Like many popular and cult movies, *Dr. No* has accrued over the years a layer of anecdotal and often apocryphal stories that are sometimes repeated as if they were documented fact. Among the more common are that *Dr. No* was a low-budget film (in fact, its budget was significantly above the average for a British first feature in the early 1960s), that Ian Fleming initially disapproved of the casting of Sean Connery as Bond (the author's published letters reveal that he met Connery prior to shooting and approved of him from the start), that in an early draft of the script, Dr. No was a monkey (an examination of the unpublished script materials reveals this is categorically untrue), and that *Dr. No* was relegated to the "sticks" in the United States (it was actually accorded a "première showcase" release by United Artists in New York and other major cities).

INTRODUCTION

One example may suffice to demonstrate how anecdote becomes accepted as fact. This is the oft-repeated story that Fleming's friend Noël Coward was offered the role of Dr. No, to which he supposedly replied by telegram: "Dear Ian—the answer to Dr. No is no, no, no, no!" It is not at all clear where this story originated: most authors who recount it do not provide a source or reference, and those who do invariably cite one of the previous unsourced accounts.[13] However, the anecdote does not feature in either the official "life" of Ian Fleming by John Pearson or in Andrew Lycett's authoritative biography. Nor does it appear in Coward's published letters.[14] This is not to say that the story is necessarily untrue; but the absence of a documented source means that it must at least be accepted with a very large pinch of salt. My view is that it has about as much claim to authenticity as Ingrid Bergman's testimony that she never knew how the last scene of *Casablanca* (1942) would play out until the day it was shot.[15]

For this book, I have looked beyond the anecdotes and drawn upon scripts, budgets, production correspondence, promotional materials, and contemporary reviews. The value of primary sources such as these is that they document the day-to-day production of the film without having to rely on the vagaries of memory. And they provide hard evidence of the contexts in which key creative decisions were made. My research has drawn upon materials held by the Wisconsin Historical Society (the corporate records of United Artists), the University of Iowa's Special Collections (the papers of Bond screenwriter Richard Maibaum), and the Special Collections Unit of the British Film Institute (which holds copies of the fourth and fifth draft

INTRODUCTION

screenplays of *Dr. No*). I have been particularly fortunate in having access to the archive of the completion guarantor Film Finances, which holds extensive production records relating to *Dr. No*, including the original financing and distribution contracts, the draft and final production budgets, a nearly complete set of daily progress reports from location shoots and the studio, and correspondence between Harry Saltzman and the guarantor as the cost situation of the film escalated alarmingly during its studio period. This material casts new light on previous (and sometimes misleading) accounts of the production of *Dr. No*, which proves to have been rather more problematic than the "official" narrative would suggest.

At the same time, this is intended to be more than just a "making of the film" book. I am also interested in the wider contexts of the production and its reception, including *Dr. No*'s historical significance for the film industry and its place in popular film culture. In this regard, I am mindful of the words of Sheldon Hall in his excellent historical study of *Zulu*:

> For a start, as both a historian and a critic I am interested in understanding how a film—any film—came to take the form that it did. This means, among other things, attempting to explore some of the contexts (social, political, industrial and commercial) within which the film was produced. With that in view, this book can be taken as a case study of *Zulu*'s historical "moment" and the various pressures acting on it—forces which I have tried, as far as possible, to present in concrete terms rather than as vague speculations.[16]

INTRODUCTION

This book may similarly be understood as an account of the "historical moment" of *Dr. No*. To that end, I have sought to consider the various industrial and cultural contexts in which it was produced as well as document the process of the making of the film. The former include the film's relationship to its source text; the production ecologies of the British and US film industries in the early 1960s; the economic and cultural strategies of United Artists; and the film's place in relation to the changing social and cultural landscape of the 1960s.

The structure of the book reflects these contexts. Chapter 1 considers the source text, exploring Ian Fleming's novel and analyzing its themes and social politics. It pays particular attention to the book's reception: *Dr. No* was the sixth James Bond adventure, but it was the first of the books to draw a storm of adverse criticism for its excesses of "sex, snobbery and sadism." Chapter 2 locates the film in the industrial contexts of the British and American film industries in the early 1960s: it includes an analysis of the financing and distribution contracts that laid the ground for the production of other early Bond films. Chapter 3 examines the scripting process that turned Fleming's book into a film. It considers the inputs of the different writers involved and explores the ideological as well as structural changes made to the novel in adapting it for the screen. Chapter 4 documents the production, drawing upon the daily progress reports and coverage in the Jamaican press. This chapter also explains the context of the "takeover" of *Dr. No* by the completion guarantor Film Finances, which intervened when it felt that Saltzman and Broccoli had lost control of the film.

INTRODUCTION

Chapter 5 explores the picture's critical and popular reception in Britain and the United States and argues that the film's popular success needs to be understood in relation to contemporary film culture. The final chapter focuses on the film itself: its social and cultural politics and its production design and visual style. It also draws upon subsequent critical readings of *Dr. No*, especially from the perspectives of gender studies and postcolonial criticism, that highlight some of the problematic content of the film.

It is my hope that this book will interest both film historians and Bond fans. For the film historian, it offers a case study of a film that is historically important but has until now been left out of the canon of those deemed worthy of a stand-alone monograph. For the Bond fan, it provides a new perspective that strips away some of the myths and received wisdoms. For both constituencies, the aim is to show that the place of *Dr. No* in the history of cinema has to do with more than just its status as "the first James Bond film."

Chapter One

SEX, SNOBBERY, AND SADISM

JAMES BOND was the creation of Ian Fleming (1908–1964), an Old Etonian, Reuters journalist, and former stockbroker who had served as personal assistant to the director of naval intelligence, Rear-Admiral John Godfrey, during the Second World War, before becoming foreign manager of the Kemsley Newspaper Group, owner of the *Sunday Times*, in 1946 (figure 1.1). It was in 1952, while Fleming was on his annual winter holiday in Jamaica, that he turned his hand to writing spy fiction. He later explained this as a form of catharsis arising from his imminent marriage to his long-term mistress, Ann Charteris: "I was about to get married—a prospect which filled me with terror and mental fidgets. To give my idle hands something to do, and as an antidote to my qualms about the marriage state after 43 years as a bachelor, I decided one day to damn well sit down and write a book."[1] The result was *Casino Royale*—intended as a "spy story to end all spy stories"—which was published by Jonathan Cape in April 1953.

In total, Fleming wrote twelve James Bond novels and two collections of short stories that were published annually between 1953 and 1966: *Casino Royale, Live and Let Die, Moonraker, Diamonds Are Forever, From Russia, with Love, Dr. No, Goldfinger, For Your Eyes Only, Thunderball, The Spy Who Loved Me, On Her Majesty's Secret Service, You Only Live Twice, The Man with the Golden Gun*, and *Octopussy and the Living Daylights*. (The last two volumes were published posthumously following Fleming's death in August 1964.) Sales of the early books were steady rather than spectacular: the first hardback edition of *Casino Royale*—now a highly prized item among book collectors—had a print run of only 4,750 copies. From 1955, however, the Bond books were also published in paperback by Pan. It was the availability of these cheaper editions that significantly broadened the character's popular appeal in Britain: combined UK sales of all of the Bond titles rose from 41,000 in 1955 to 58,000 in 1956, 72,000 in 1957, 105,000 in 1958, 237,000 in 1959, and 323,000 in 1960.[2] In 1957, *From Russia, with Love* became the first of the books to be serialized in a mass-circulation newspaper (the *Daily Express*). The Bond books were a major landmark in the publishing of popular fiction, according to literary historian John Sutherland, who sees them as "a breakthrough comparable in some ways to [Penguin Books founder Allen] Lane's, thirty years earlier." He amplifies that the "importance of the Bond books was that they revealed a new reliable market for a certain kind of book that was not trash and could be marketed as a 'brand name' (i.e. 'the latest Bond')."[3]

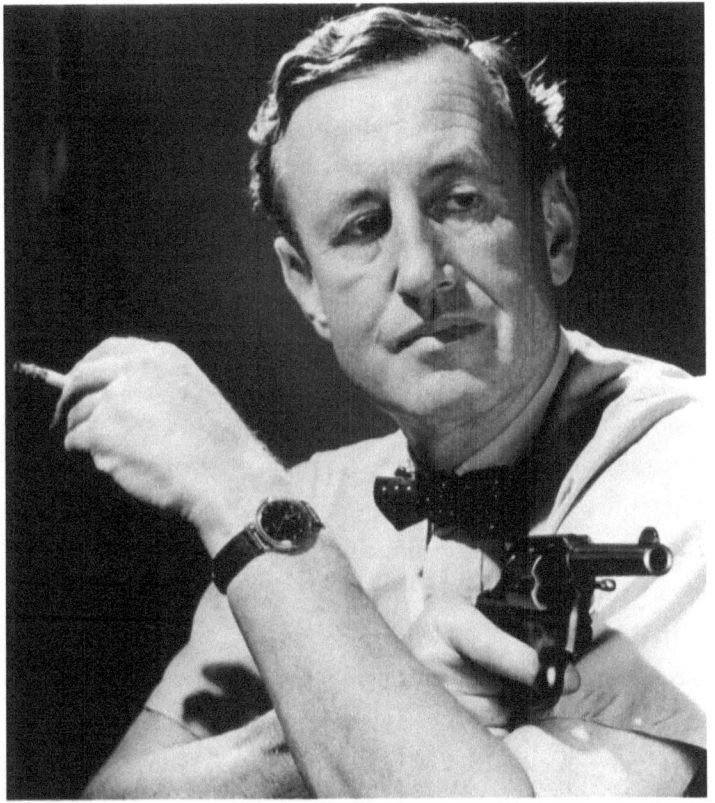

FIGURE 1.1 A publicity shot of Ian Fleming in a suitably Bondian pose, early 1960s. Courtesy of the Everett Collection/Alamy.

The early Bond books were initially well received by the book-reviewing fraternity in Britain. Most reviewers regarded them as superior entertainments, polished thrillers with a sophisticated veneer. Alan Ross (*Times Literary Supplement*), for example, found *Casino Royale* "an extremely engaging affair, dealing with espionage in the 'Sapper' manner, but with a hero who, although taking a great many cold showers and never letting sex interfere with his work, is somewhat more sophisticated... Altogether Mr. Fleming has produced a book that is both exciting and extremely civilized."[4] Simon Raven (*The Listener*) described the same book as "a kind of supersonic John Buchan" and praised Fleming "for taking the best elements of the [Peter] Cheyney method (speed, controlled savagery, a pungent and sceptical idiom) and yet combining them with the more spacious and gracious atmosphere of old-style international intrigue—monocles, medals, and milor-dos."[5] The response to the early books seems to have suggested that they succeeded because they were written as unpretentious entertainment. George W. Bishop (*Daily Telegraph*) felt that *Live and Let Die* "is continually exciting... and is the more entertaining because Mr. Fleming does not take it all too seriously himself."[6] And *Moonraker*, he wrote, was "[a] fantastic piece of romance. I didn't believe a word of it, but I couldn't put the book down until it was finished."[7] Raymond Chandler (*Sunday Times*) proclaimed *Diamonds Are Forever* "about the nicest piece of book-writing in this type of literature which I have seen for a long time."[8] Julian Symons (*Times Literary Supplement*) averred that Fleming "has done something for, or to, the post-war thriller; the something is not very nice, perhaps, but it brings the thriller into line with modern emotional needs... *From Russia, With Love* is Mr. Fleming's tautest, most exciting and most brilliant tale."[9]

Fleming's Bond books hold an important place in the history of British spy fiction, a genre that emerged in the early twentieth century and has been understood as a mirror for the changing political and social landscape of Britain. Fleming was the last of the "old school" thriller writers: his books span the gap between the pre–Second World War adventure stories of authors such as John Buchan and "Sapper"—both of whom were cited as points of reference in the reviews of *Casino Royale*—and the more realistic spy stories of the 1960s by Len Deighton and John le Carré. On the one hand, Bond is something of an ideological throwback: his vintage Bentley and his specially blended cigarettes by "Morlands of Grosvenor Street" locate him in a tradition of patriotic gentleman heroes extending back to Buchan's Richard Hannay and Sapper's Bulldog Drummond.[10] Fleming's parade of grotesque master criminals—Le Chiffre, Mr. Big, Sir Hugo Drax, Dr. No, Auric Goldfinger, and Ernst Stavro Blofeld—belong to the same brotherhood of supervillains as Buchan's Dominic Medina and Sapper's Carl Petersen. On the other hand, Bond differs from the former gentleman amateurs insofar as he is a professional secret agent with a "licence to kill." An oft-quoted reflection by Bond at the beginning of *Goldfinger* sums up his role as a licensed assassin:

> It was part of his profession to kill people. He had never liked doing it and when he had to kill he did it as well as he knew how and forgot about it. As a secret agent who held the rare double-O prefix—the licence to kill in the Secret Service—it was his duty to be as cool about death as a surgeon.[11]

Bond is also characterized as a social outsider rather than a clubman such as Hannay or Drummond. As he reflects while visiting the exclusive dinner-and-gambling club Blades in *Moonraker*: "Bond knew that there was something alien and un-English about himself. He knew that he was a difficult man to cover up."[12]

Like all popular fiction, the Bond stories are tracts for their times. They are informed by and respond to—whether consciously or unconsciously—the political, social, and cultural contexts in which they were written and consumed. The Soviet-backed antagonists of the books between *Casino Royale* and *For Your Eyes Only*—with the sole exception of *Diamonds Are Forever*, where Bond is pitted against American gangsters known as the Spangled Mob—locate Fleming's hero in the ideological and cultural contexts of the Cold War. The series rehearses a Manichean world view in which the West is associated with the values of liberal democracy—Bond's recurring allies include Felix Leiter of the CIA (and later, Pinkerton's Detective Agency) and René Mathis of the Deuxième Bureau—while the Soviet Union and its allies represent an enemy with totalitarian beliefs. Only in the first book is the ideological certainty of the Cold War questioned. Bond reflects at one point that "this country right-or-wrong business is getting a little out-of-date . . . History is moving pretty quickly these days and the heroes and villains keep on changing parts." Even then, his doubt is only temporary: Bond finds a purpose in combating the insidious Soviet counterespionage agency known as SMERSH (*Smiert Spionam*—"Death to Spies").[13]

The Bond books are also set against the background of social and political changes in postwar Britain. This was a period when the nation's influence was in decline: its world power status was challenged by the geopolitical might of the United States and the Soviet Union, and the process of decolonization that had begun with independence for India and Pakistan in 1947 accelerated from the late 1950s as Britain relinquished much of its overseas empire. David Cannadine points out the (entirely coincidental) symbolism in the publication history of the Bond books: *Casino Royale* preceded by a few weeks the Coronation of Queen Elizabeth II in 1953, "a retrospectively unconvincing reaffirmation of Britain's continued great-power status," while the last full novel, *The Man with the Golden Gun*, was published in April 1965, a few months after the funeral of Sir Winston Churchill, an event that not only represented "the last rites of the great man himself, but was also self-consciously recognised as being a requiem for Britain as a great power."[14] The books written after the Suez Crisis of 1956 increasingly began to include references to the decline of British power and the retreat from empire. The three set in Jamaica—*Live and Let Die*, *Dr. No*, and *The Man with the Golden Gun*—include reflections on the transition from British colonial rule to independence.[15]

Dr. No was Fleming's sixth Bond novel and marked something of a turning point for the series. Following *Casino Royale*, a taut counterespionage thriller that was both narratively and psychologically plausible, the agent's adventures had become increasingly more sensational and far-fetched. In his essay on the Bond books, Umberto Eco suggests that after *Casino Royale*, Fleming "renounces all psychology as the motive of narrative and decides to transfer characters and situations to the level of an objective and conventional structural strategy."[16] The following books had featured such elements as an African-American underworld kingpin selling gold doubloons to finance Soviet espionage activities in the United States (*Live and Let Die*), a fanatical ex-Nazi who plots to destroy London with a nuclear missile (*Moonraker*), an American mobster with his own private railroad (*Diamonds Are Forever*), and an implausibly elaborate conspiracy to lure Bond to his death on the Orient Express (*From Russia, with Love*). Fleming had toyed with the idea of killing off his hero at the end of the latter book, which ends on a cliff-hanger as Bond collapses after being stabbed by Rosa Klebb's poison-spiked shoe. At the time, Fleming confided in his friend William Plomer: "My greatest fear is staleness. It is so difficult to communicate zest if it isn't there, and though I still enjoy writing about Bond, I constantly find myself piling on adjectives (as you sapiently note) to fill the vacuum created by my waning enthusiasm for this cardboard booby."[17]

The origin of *Dr. No* was in a treatment for a television series whose working title had been *James Gunn—Secret Agent*: this had been commissioned from Fleming by the US producer Henry Morgenthau III (son of the country's former treasury secretary) in September 1956. Fleming's synopsis revolved around an ongoing battle of wits between the titular hero and "an international freelance spy of Chinese-German extraction."[18] Fleming was never one to let a good plot go to waste, so when the planned series did not go ahead, he used the story as the basis for his sixth Bond adventure. *Dr. No* was the most far-fetched of the books to date: the agent is pitted against a diabolical megalomaniac called Dr. Julius No whose guano factory on a private island in the Caribbean turns out to be the cover for a radio beam which he is using to interfere with

American missile tests from a nearby base on Turks Island. Bond is assisted by faithful Cayman Islander Quarrel (a character who had previously appeared in *Live and Let Die*) and by a "Girl Tarzan" known as Honeychile Rider whom he meets on Dr. No's island where she is collecting valuable seashells. Among the more preposterous incidents of the book are Bond's battle with Dr. No's "dragon" (a marsh buggy armed with a flame-thrower) and his fight with a giant squid, which seems to have strayed into the book from *Twenty Thousand Leagues under the Sea*. Dr. No himself was Fleming's most megalomaniac and demonic villain yet: this fiendish Oriental mastermind threatening the security of the West was nothing if not a throwback to Sax Rohmer's Dr. Fu Manchu, the "Yellow Peril," who had appeared in a series of books and films beginning in 1913.[19]

An anecdote about the writing of *Dr. No* exemplifies the attention to detail that Fleming brought to the Bond books. Following *Diamonds Are Forever*, he had been contacted by a small-arms expert named Geoffrey Boothroyd, who wrote:

> I have, by now, got rather fond of Mr. James Bond. I like most of the things about him, with the exception of his rather deplorable taste in firearms. In particular I dislike a man who comes into contact with all sorts of formidable people using a .25 Beretta. That sort of gun is really a lady's gun, and not a really nice lady at that.[20]

Fleming took Boothroyd's criticism to heart: chapter 2 of *Dr. No* ("Choice of Weapons") sees Bond obliged to relinquish his trusty

Beretta in preference for a Walther PPK 7.65-millimeter and a Smith & Wesson Centennial Airweight (which the author confused with the heavier Smith & Wesson .357 Magnum and dropped from later books). Fleming named the Secret Service armorer Major Boothroyd and gave him the "ladies' gun" line.[21]

Dr. No prompted a more divisive critical reaction than Fleming's previous books. Most reviewers found it to be in much the same literary vein as its predecessors, only even more improbable. Peter John Stead (*Times Literary Supplement*) felt that only this particular writer could have succeeded with such a fantastical plot: "Mr. Ian Fleming's mastery of the Secret Service thriller has encouraged him to offer too opulent a feast in *Dr. No*. A less accomplished writer, lacking Mr. Fleming's quick descriptive gift and his power of making his characters talk with such lucid and natural style, would never have got away with this story."[22] Violet Grant (*Daily Telegraph*) concurred insofar as *Dr. No* revealed the author "at the top of his form" and wrote that "Mr. Fleming's amazing imagination shows no sign of flagging. But is not the sinister German-Chinese Dr. No, with his articulated steel hands, getting dangerously near the fantastic and incredible?"[23] And Raymond Chandler felt that the plot "not only borders on fantasy, it plunges into it with both feet." But the creator of Philip Marlowe also felt that the qualities he admired in Fleming—his "escape from mandarin English" and his "acute sense of pace"—had reached maturity: "What has happened to him in *Dr. No* is what happens to every real thriller writer. He has found that a novel, a thriller, or what you choose to call it, is a world, that it has its own depth and subtleties, and that these can be expressed in an offhand way, without calling attention to themselves and be very much alive."[24]

However, there were other critics who deplored *Dr. No*, seeing it as an extreme case of the "snobbery with violence" tradition of British sensational thriller fiction. Bernard Bergonzi (*The Twentieth Century*) launched a broadside against Fleming in which he noted "a strongly marked streak of voyeurism and sado-masochism" in the Bond books and deplored "the complete lack of any ethical frame of reference." Bergonzi described the "erotic fantasies" of the books as those of "a dirty-minded schoolboy" and complained that Fleming "describes scenes of violence with uncommon relish." In contrast to critics who regarded Bond as a sophisticated modern hero, he felt that the books revealed "an air of vulgarity and display which contrast strongly with those subdued images of the perfectly self-assured gentlemanly lifestyle that we find in Buchan or even Sapper." Bergonzi concluded that the popularity of the books was evidence of moral turpitude and a society that was losing touch with its traditional values: "Mr. Fleming, I imagine, knows just what he is doing, but the fact that his books are published by a very reputable firm, and are regularly reviewed—and highly praised—in our self-respecting intellectual weeklies, surely says more about the present state of our culture than a whole volume of abstract denunciations."[25]

Other attacks followed. Paul Johnson (*New Statesman*), headlining his review "Sex, Snobbery and Sadism," averred that *Dr. No* was "without doubt the nastiest book I have ever read." He wrote: "There are three basic ingredients in *Dr. No*, all unhealthy, all thoroughly English: the sadism of a schoolboy bully, the mechanical, two-dimensional sex longings of a frustrated adolescent, and the crude snob-cravings of a suburban adult." To add insult to injury, he also declared that Fleming "has no literary skill" and that the book was "badly written to the point of incoherence." Johnson related *Dr. No* to a previous *cause célèbre* of sensational crime fiction, citing George Orwell's critique of James Hadley Chase's notorious *No Orchids for Miss Blandish*, and concluded that Bond's popularity was an outcome of changing social values in Britain: "Our curious post-war society, with its obsessive interest in debutantes, its cult of U and non-U, its working-class graduates educated into snobbery by the welfare state, is a soft market for Mr. Fleming's poison."[26] The *Manchester Guardian* published a leading article that similarly deplored "the cult of luxury for its own sake" and the "pernicious" brand-name snobbery of the books, though it let Fleming off the hook on the grounds that "since the reader is plainly expected to identify himself with Bond, these works are symptomatic of a decline in taste. However, if that is so, it is the readers who are to blame; and to call down thunder upon the head of Bond or his creator is the sign of a guilty conscience."[27]

The ideological critiques of Fleming's books by a section of the literati locate them within a contemporary social and political debate over the "state of the nation." On the one hand, the 1950s have often been characterized as a decade of conservatism and consensus. The esteem in which the monarchy was held and the personal popularity of Winston Churchill, reelected as Prime Minister in 1951, may be seen as evidence of the former. The latter was exemplified in the emergence of "Butskellism"—a term used to describe the common ground between the progressive wing of the Conservative Party (exemplified by Chancellor of the Exchequer R. A. Butler) and the moderate center-left Labour Party (led by Hugh Gaitskell)—and the existence of an ideological consensus over matters ranging from defense policy to the welfare state.[28] On the other hand, the later part of the decade saw the emergence of an oppositional trend in British culture and politics that took various forms, from the "Angry Young Men"—labelled as such following John Osborne's play *Look Back in Anger*, first performed at the Royal Court Theatre in 1956—to the founding of the Campaign for Nuclear Disarmament in 1958 and the publication of the *New Left Review* beginning in 1959. There was a view on the intellectual left (shared by some on the intellectual right) that British society had become moribund and was in a state of decline. In the eyes of Fleming's critics, James Bond was a symptom of everything that was wrong with 1950s Britain: its political conservatism, its social elitism, its materialistic culture, and its attachment to an outmoded imperial identity.

So, how fair were the charges of "sex, snobbery and sadism" levelled against *Dr. No*? On the first count, it would be fair to say that *Dr. No* is no more and no less explicit than the other Bond books in its sexual content. Some contemporary critics averred that the content of the series bordered on the pornographic: sequences such as the performance of the striptease artiste in *Live and Let Die* and the fight between two gypsy girls in *From Russia, with Love* were written for titillation rather than to serve any real narrative function. Fleming's descriptions of women present them as erotic objects: the physical feature most frequently described are their "fine," "firm," "proud," or "splendid" breasts.[29] In his book *The Neophiliacs*, Christopher Booker states that the Bond novels reflected the increasing visibility of sex in postwar Britain, which

> was not just a concern with the realities of sex; even more, it was a preoccupation with the idea of sex, the image of sex; the written word, the visual image, the image that was promulgated in advertisements, in increasingly "daring" films, in "controversial" newspaper articles and "frank" novels; the image purveyed by the strip-tease clubs and pornographic shops that were springing up in the back streets of Soho and provincial cities; and the image that, mixed with that of violence, was responsible in the years after 1956 for the enormous boom in the sales of Ian Fleming's James Bond stories.[30]

In this context, the Bond books may be aligned with British new wave films such as *Room at the Top* (1959)—advertised as "a savage story of lust and ambition"—as well as the continental "sex films" shown in private cinema clubs. Fleming himself once remarked that "the target of my books . . . lay somewhere between the solar plexus and, well, the upper thigh."[31]

The erotic interest of *Dr. No* is focused entirely on the character of Honeychile Rider, whose first appearance is described thus:

> It was a naked girl, with her back to him. She was not quite naked. She wore a broad leather belt around her waist with

a hunting knife in a leather sheath at her right hip. The belt made her nakedness extraordinarily erotic . . . She stood in the classical relaxed pose of the nude, all the weight on the right leg and the left knee bent and turning slightly inwards, the head to one side as she examined the things in her hand.[32]

This is a characteristic motif of the books (not just *Dr. No*), in which "the girl" is described from Bond's point of view and is initially unaware that she is the object of his gaze. Michael Denning has argued that the Bond books can be seen as a form of voyeuristic spectacle: the agent not only carries a "licence to kill" but also bears a "licence to look." In this reading, "Bond's pornographic imagination is structured not so much around sexual acts as around Bond as voyeur."[33] The privileging of the male point of view in this scene empowers the male reader and represents the woman as a sexualized object. Indeed "the girl" in *Dr. No* is literally compared to a painting: she stands "in the classical relaxed pose of the nude" and later in the same passage Bond compares her mentally to "Botticelli's Venus, seen from behind."[34]

There is certainly a fetishistic quality in Fleming's writing. One manifestation of this is that "the girl" is often damaged in some way. This may take the form of sexual trauma—Tiffany Case (*Diamonds Are Forever*) and Pussy Galore (*Goldfinger*) are both victims of rape—or a physical deformity, such as that of Domino Vitali (*Thunderball*), who limps because one leg is an inch shorter than the other. *Dr. No* includes the most extreme example of this tendency, insofar as Honeychile has a broken nose she sustained in attempting to defend herself from sexual assault. Bond is initially horrified by her injury (he "stiffened with revolt at what had happened to this supremely beautiful girl"), but in the course of the book comes to accept it ("She looked ravishing . . . Now Bond loved the broken nose. It had become part of his thoughts of her and it suddenly occurred to him that he would be sad when she was just an immaculately beautiful girl like other beautiful girls").[35] In other respects, Honeychile is atypical of Fleming's heroines. She is around twenty, younger than usual, and she is much less worldly than other characters such as Vesper Lynd (*Casino Royale*) or Tiffany Case. Bond's attitude toward her is more protective than predatory: he resolves to arrange an operation for her nose and even to find a job for her. Indeed, it is Honeychile who makes clear her attraction to Bond: he feels obliged to resist her advances on several occasions ("What about the physical desire he felt for her? One could not make love to a child") until he sleeps with her at the end to fulfil a promise (she commands: "Take off those and come in. You promised. You owe me slave-time.").[36]

The charge of snobbery rests largely on Bond's preference for expensive brand-name consumer goods—his Rolex Oyster Perpetual wristwatch, his Jamaican Blue Mountain coffee, his Sea Island cotton shirts—and his taste for good food and fine wines. In fact, *Dr. No* features less of the snobbery around food and wine that characterizes other books such as *Casino Royale* or *Moonraker*. Like all world-class supervillains, Dr. No entertains Bond at dinner: the menu cards "might have been from the Savoy Grill, or the '21', or the Tour d'Argent. It began with *Caviar de Beluga* and ended with *Sorbet à la Champagne*."[37] Otherwise, the only real instance of the cult of luxury is the "mink-lined prison" in which Bond and Honeychile are kept before meeting Dr. No ("Floris Lime bath essence for men and Guerlain bathcubes for women") and here, the expensive consumables have been chosen by the villain. In *The James Bond Dossier* (still by far the most accessible and perceptive critique of Fleming's books), Kingsley Amis would defend Fleming's use of brand-name items on the grounds that they provided a sense of verisimilitude: "He names things to provide a linkage with reality, very desirable when the plot and much else is non-realistic; to appeal where possible to our own experience; to act as shorthand in sketching in a character or milieu; and to encourage our sense of participation."[38] Fleming himself defended Bond's branded goods on much the same lines: "[To] create an illusion of depth I had to fit Bond out with some theatrical props and, while I kept his wardrobe as discreet as his personality, I did equip him with a distinctive gun and, though they are a security hazard, with distinctive cigarettes... The gimmickry grew like bind-weed and now, while it still amuses me, it has become an unfortunate trademark."[39]

The charge of sadism perhaps has more substance. In most of the Bond books, Fleming devised imaginative if gruesome scenes where the hero is subjected to diabolical torture by his enemies: having his genitals whipped with a carpet beater (*Casino Royale*), being hauled over a sharp coral reef (*Live and Let Die*), being burned by steam hoses (*Moonraker*), and being beaten by heavies wearing football boots (*Diamonds Are Forever*). *Dr. No* features the most extreme physical ordeal for Bond to date: he is faced with a fiendish obstacle course that involves crawling through a ventilation system where he experiences electric shocks, heat burns, and a cage full of poisonous spiders, culminating in an encounter with a giant squid. The purpose of this is not to extract information but rather to test his physical courage and endurance. Dr. No is the most extreme manifestation of the sadean tendency that characterizes all of Fleming's villains. He tells Bond and Honeychile:

> I am interested in pain. I am also interested in finding out how much the human body can endure. From time to time I make experiments on those of my people who have to be punished. And on trespassers like yourselves. You have both put me to a great deal of trouble. In exchange I intend to put you to a great deal of pain. I shall record the length of your endurance. The facts will be noted. One day my findings will be given to the world. Your deaths will have served the purposes of science. I never waste human material.[40]

Bond's torture ordeal was foreshadowed at the beginning of the novel, where "the famous neurologist" Sir James Maloney advises M, head of the Secret Service, that "there are limits to a man's courage" and tells him that "pain's an odd thing. We know very little about it. You can't measure it—the difference in suffering between a woman having a baby and a man having a renal colic."[41] In this sense, Dr. No's sadistic experiment is Fleming's way of answering the theoretical question posed at the beginning of the book.

Contemporary commentators tended to attribute Fleming's torture scenes to an excess of writerly imagination. As the reviewer of *The Times* remarked of *Dr. No*: "Hitherto a highbrow vogue has emphasized the literary qualities of the Bond books. They are undoubtedly most professional, but their appeal has its much simpler and much nastier side . . . Mr. Fleming is up against the appetite he feeds—no torture can quite satisfy the schoolboy pride in devising one's own yet more exquisitely loathsome Room 101."[42] Amis—citing *Casino Royale*—suggested that "a very well-established and basic element of the thriller story is at work" in the torture scene, which "makes us feel admiration and sympathy for the hero and fear and hatred for the villain."[43] Alex Adams has argued that a more ideological process is at work: that the tortures endured by Bond have less to do with any masochistic impulse than with asserting his moral and physical superiority over his enemies. In this reading, the agent's resistance to pain reinforces "hegemonic masculinity" and presents Bond himself as "an image of elite power which circulates at a time of international decline." *Dr. No* fits this narrative particularly well, as it is located in an outpost of the British Empire and the villain represents a foreign threat to the imperial body politic.[44] However, Bond is able to negotiate the diabolical obstacle course and overcomes the worst tortures the villain has been able to devise. In the process, he reasserts the vitality of British rule at a time of increasing real-world challenges to British power.

Amis exonerates Fleming of the charge of sadism: he considers the violence of the books to fall mostly within the parameters of "legitimate excitement and horror."[45] He compares Bond to Mike Hammer, the tough American private eye created by Mickey Spillane, and points out that, unlike Hammer, Bond does not inflict wanton or gratuitous violence on others.

Fleming's Bond, for example, never strikes a woman in the course of the books. However, the same observation does not apply to other characters. *Dr. No* includes several moments where violence is overlaid with a notably misogynistic streak: the murder of Mary Trueblood is sadistic ("The man smiled broadly. Slowly, lovingly, he lifted the gun and shot her three times in and around the left breast"), and Quarrel seems to relish hurting Dr. No's agent Annabel Chung when he marks her by squeezing the "Mount of Venus" in her hand.[46] Honeychile is also a victim of sexual violence: she tells Bond quite matter-of-factly about the occasion she was raped by "a man called Mander" and exacted retribution by putting a Black Widow spider in his bed. She is, however, spared the gruesome fate planned for her by Dr. No: he has her staked out in the path of giant crabs, expecting they will eat her alive, but it turns out that the crabs have no taste for human flesh and Honeychile is able to escape. Nevertheless the threat as described by Dr. No is both sexualized and racialized: "It is a year since I put a girl to death in the fashion I have chosen for you, woman. She was a Negress. She lasted three hours. She died of terror. I have wanted a white girl for comparison."[47]

Contemporary critics seem to have been rather less bothered about the racial politics of *Dr. No* than other aspects of the book. This may have been because racist ideology is structurally embedded in the British thriller tradition to the extent of becoming normalized. John G. Cawelti explains how the politics of the thriller take an explicitly racialized form:

> The British Empire and its white Christian civilization are constantly in danger of subversion by villains who represent

other races or racial mixtures. Saxe [*sic*] Rohmer's Fu Manchu and his hordes of little yellow and brown conspirators against the purity and safety of English society are only an extreme example of the pervasive racial symbolism of this period.[48]

The Bond books conform to this pattern: the characterizations of African Americans (*Live and Let Die*) and Koreans (*Goldfinger*) are crude stereotypes, while even apparently British villains such as Sir Hugo Drax (*Moonraker*) and Auric Goldfinger turn out to be naturalized foreigners. *Dr. No* is a particularly extreme example of Fleming's racial imaginary: the titular villain is "the only son of a German Methodist missionary and a Chinese girl of good family" and his men are described as "Chigroes" (a contraction of "Chinese Negroes" that William Plomer suggested after reading the manuscript).[49] Fleming's description of this caste, through the mouth of Colonial Secretary Pleydell-Smith, is an especially ungracious example of racial stereotyping: "The Chigroes are a tough, forgotten race. They look down on the Negroes and the Chinese look down on them. One day they may become a nuisance. They've got some of the intelligence of the Chinese and most of the vices of the black man."[50]

At the same time, the racism of *Dr. No* is peculiarly selective. For example, it does not extend to the character of Quarrel, the Cayman Islander who takes the role of Bond's local ally and for whom Bond feels genuine affection. Quarrel has the "warm dry" handshake that is invariably an indicator of a good man in Fleming's world, and "dark grey eyes that showed descent from a Cromwellian soldier or a pirate of Morgan's time."[51] He is deferential toward Bond ("Okay, cap'n" is his most frequent comment), but Bond treats him as an equal. (Quarrel had previously appeared in *Live and Let Die*, where the men's relationship was compared to "that of a Scots laird with his head stalker: authority was unspoken and there was no room for servility.")[52] Bond is genuinely upset when Quarrel is killed (horribly) in the battle with Dr. No's marsh buggy. In the last chapter, he reflects on the death of his friend: "Bond thought of the burned twist down in the swamp that had been Quarrel. He remembered the soft ways of the big body, the innocence in the grey, horizon-seeking eyes, the simple lusts and desires, the reverence for superstitions and instincts, the childish faults, the loyalty and even love that Quarrel had given him—the warmth, there was only one word for it, of the man."[53]

The politics of race in *Dr. No* cannot be detached from its representation of colonialism. The novel is notably inaccurate in its description of the political structures of colonial Jamaica. It was written shortly after the departure of Sir Hugh Foot, governor of Jamaica between 1951 and 1957. It presents a top-down structure of colonial government where the unnamed acting governor exercises political authority: in reality Jamaica had been moving toward self-government since the Second World War and the elected prime minister had been the effective head of government since 1955. The novel is replete with reminders of Jamaica's colonial past ("Bond almost smelled the dung of the mule train in which he would have been riding over from Port Royal to visit the garrison at Morgan's Harbour in 1750") and the institutions of British rule. The governor's office at King's House symbolizes British monarchical authority ("From one end of the room King George VI, from the other end the Queen, looked down the table with grace and good humour").[54] Fleming, again through Pleydell-Smith, describes Jamaican society in terms that acknowledge the exploitative nature of colonialism while at the same time reinforcing its racist underpinnings:

> The Jamaican is a kindly lazy man with the virtues and vices of a child. He lives on a very rich island but he doesn't get rich from it. He doesn't know how to and he's too lazy. The British come and go and take the easy pickings, but for about two hundred years no Englishman has made a fortune out here. He doesn't stay long enough. He takes a fat cut and leaves. It's the Portuguese Jews who make the most. They came here with the British and they've stayed. But they're snobs and they spend all of their fortunes on building fine houses and giving dances ... Then come the Syrians, very rich too, but not such good businessmen. They have most of the stores and some of the best hotels. They're not a very good risk. Get overstocked and have to have an occasional fire to get liquid again. Then there are the Indians with their usual flashy trade in soft goods and the like. They're not much of a lot. Finally there are the Chinese, solid, compact, discreet—the most powerful clique in Jamaica. They've got the bakeries and the laundries and the best food stores. They keep to themselves and keep their strain pure.[55]

Despite the extreme ethnic stereotyping, this is a not entirely inaccurate picture of Jamaica at the time. While the Chinese community was a small minority (seventy thousand of a total population of over 1.6 million in 1960), they owned over 90 percent of the island's shops, restaurants, and laundries.⁵⁶ There was a history of anti-Chinese riots in Jamaica before the war, and reports of continued racial tension were a feature of the local press during the 1950s and 1960s.

Dr. No was written after the Suez Crisis had rudely demonstrated that Britain was no longer able to act independently to assert its global strategic interests. It is the first of the series to cast some doubt on the institutions of British colonialism. The book opens at Queen's Club ("the social Mecca of Kingston"). Fleming's prediction of the end of British rule ("Such stubborn retreats will not long survive in modern Jamaica. One day Queen's Club will have its windows smashed and perhaps be burned to the ground") presages the violent disruption of the social order when three "blind" beggars assassinate Commander John Strangways, the senior Secret Service officer in the Caribbean.⁵⁷ In other respects, *Dr. No* sets up a contrast between the incompetent and resentful acting governor, who wants to brush Strangways's disappearance under the carpet ("This man's been passed over for the Governor-Generalship of Rhodesia. Now all he wants is to retire and get some directorships in the City. Last thing he wants is any trouble in Jamaica") and the professionalism of the military ("The Brigadier in command of the Caribbean Defence Force was a modern young soldier of thirty-five. His military record was good enough for him to be unimpressed by relics from the Edwardian era of Colonial Governors, whom he collectively referred to as 'feather-hatted fuddy duddies'").⁵⁸ The attitude toward colonialism in *Dr. No* and the

Bond books generally is best described as one of pragmatic conservatism: Fleming recognized that the age of empire was coming to an end and believed that professional governance would smooth the path to independence. In the last full Bond novel, *The Man with the Golden Gun*, Fleming was more sanguine about the colonial legacy: "For all her new-found 'Independence' he would bet his bottom dollar that the statue of Queen Victoria in the centre of Kingston had not been destroyed or removed to a museum as similar relics of an historic infancy had been in the resurgent African states."[59]

The critical assault on *Dr. No* from certain critics did nothing to harm its popularity. The first edition of the hardback had a print run of twenty thousand (five thousand more than *From Russia, with Love*) and it was also serialized in the *Daily Express*. The first paperback printing, in 1960, sold 115,000 copies in its first year. By this time, Fleming was on the cusp of the bestseller stakes that so far had eluded him. Indeed, the critical backlash against *Dr. No* was perhaps to some extent an outcome of Bond's growing popularity: a series that had hitherto been understood by the literati as a parody of the thriller was taken more seriously as its readership increased. It was also from the late 1950s on that the film industry, which had previously been unenthusiastic, began to show an interest.

Fleming, for his part, had mixed views about adapting the books into other media. On the one hand, he was interested in the commercial opportunities that film offered, but on the other, he was keen not to dumb down the Bond brand. A letter to publisher Wren Howard about the *James Bond* comic strip published by the *Daily Express* from 1958 is revealing in this regard:

"If I was a bit more hard-boiled it would be easy to guy the whole Bond operation in a great splurge of promotion and sales, but somehow it all goes against the grain a bit and I dare say much the same problem faces authors whose books are made into a lot of films."[60] However, following several abortive initiatives—including the sale of the film rights of *Casino Royale* to producer Gregory Ratoff in 1955, the Rank Organization taking an option on *Moonraker*, and an unfulfilled collaborative venture between Fleming and producer Kevin McClory to develop a film entitled *James Bond of the Secret Service* from an original screen story in the late 1950s—Fleming sold an option on all the Bond titles except *Casino Royale* to producer Harry Saltzman in 1960. And it would be *Dr. No* that was chosen to be the first James Bond film.

Chapter Two

EVERYTHING OR NOTHING

IT HAS BECOME part of the popular folklore of the Bond films that the name of production company Eon Productions stood for "Everything or Nothing."[1] This is very probably a case of retrospective attribution rather than a strict matter of historical record: contemporary sources make no reference to Eon as an acronym and Cubby Broccoli always maintained that there was no truth in the story. However, the persistence of "Everything or Nothing" is one of the many myths and half-truths that have accumulated around the origin of the James Bond film series. Most of the existing accounts are based largely on anecdotal evidence that is not always very reliable and is often contradictory. As early as 1987, in the second volume of his history of United Artists, Tino Balio drew upon the company's legal and financial records to provide an account that debunked some of the more common misconceptions.[2] Even so, the dominant narrative around *Dr. No*—that it was a risky proposition whose commercial success surprised everyone except the producers themselves—remains pervasive.

Eon and its Swiss-incorporated parent company Danjaq SA were jointly owned by producers Albert R. Broccoli (universally known as "Cubby") and Harry Saltzman (figure 2.1). New Yorker Broccoli had resided in Britain since the early 1950s. He had been a partner with Irving Allen in Warwick Film Productions, a British-based production unit that turned out a series of action-adventure pictures for distribution by Columbia Pictures, including *The Red Beret* (1953), *Hell Below Zero* (1954), *The Black Knight* (1954), *A Prize of Gold* (1955), *The Cockleshell Heroes* (1955), *Safari* (1956), *Zarak* (1956), *Fire Down Below* (1957), *Interpol* (1957), *No Time to Die* (1958), *The Bandit of Zhobe* (1959), and *Killers of Kilimanjaro* (1959). These were dual-budget pictures in

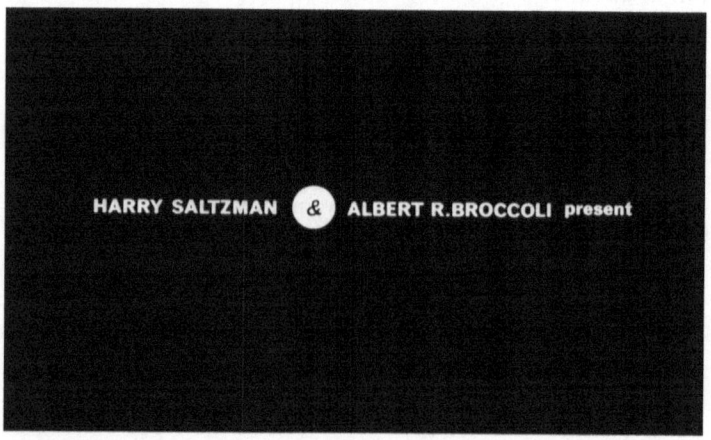

FIGURE 2.1 Eon Productions was a partnership between Harry Saltzman and Albert R. Broccoli. *Dr. No* (Danjaq LLC/United Artists Corporation, 1962).

which the Hollywood parent company provided a dollar budget that covered the "above the line" costs of script, producers' fees, and star salaries—the Warwick films usually featured American stars such as Alan Ladd, Victor Mature, and Richard Widmark—while a pounds sterling budget covering the "below the line" costs, including the production unit salaries, supporting cast, and location and studio expenses, would be raised locally. The budgets of Warwick's films ranged between £176,328 for *The Red Beret* and £297,728 for *The Black Knight*: this placed them in the higher-cost range for British first features in the 1950s but made them less expensive than equivalent films made in Hollywood.[3]

This company's output exemplified the trend toward "runaway" production in the 1950s: American-financed films shot abroad in order to benefit from lower production costs and to take advantage of local subsidies. The context for Warwick's British-based operation was the existence of the British Film Production Fund. This fund—popularly known as the Eady levy after Second Secretary to the Treasury Sir Wilfrid Eady—had been introduced in 1950 as a means of increasing the revenues received by producers of British films.[4] It was raised through a levy on all motion-picture ticket sales and yielded around £3 million a year throughout the 1950s. The levy was distributed to producers of eligible British films in proportion to the distributor's receipts: it therefore amounted in effect to a subsidy for commercial success, as it was the biggest box-office films that benefited most. The US Motion Picture Export Association estimated that the "Eady bonus" could be worth up to an additional 40 percent on the distributor's receipts of a

British-made film.[5] The eligibility criteria were the same as for the British quota (the minimum amount of British film footage that British exhibitors were required to show each year): that the film should be produced by a British-registered production company with the interiors shot in a studio in Britain or the British Commonwealth and a minimum of 80 percent of labor costs paid to British or Commonwealth citizens. The labor costs could exclude one actor and one senior technician (such as the director or writer): this allowed producers to employ American stars whose fees would be excluded from the statutory costs of the films.

Warwick Film Productions was set up in 1952 specifically for the purpose of producing in Britain. Around half of its films were made by British directors—including Terence Young, John Gilling, and Ken Hughes—and the films made extensive use of British cast and crew members. Allen and Broccoli maintained that, as independent producers, they were best placed to make films that accorded with the tastes of cinemagoers: "The public is becoming more and more discriminating, demanding better entertainment, and the studios—and distributors—are realising that a wholesale, conveyor belt line-up cannot satisfy that demand." Evidence that their production philosophy ("We have no time for message films . . . Entertainment is the thing: we strive to make films for the people who support the cinema; not those who go to the pictures about once or twice a year") was successful can be seen insofar as their films regularly featured in the top ten box-office listings of the year.[6] As R. H. "Josh" Billings, film reviews editor of the trade paper *Kine Weekly*, observed: "No doubt about it, Warwick Films . . .

certainly know the shortest cut to the box office. So far, all their runners have been winners."[7]

Warwick hit on a successful formula: the production of British films whose war, thriller, safari, and similar subject matter did not seem parochially British and had international appeal. The US trade journal *Boxoffice* averred that *The Red Beret*—retitled *Paratrooper* for release in the United States and Canada—had star and production values "to guarantee grosses in the American market that substantially transcend those accorded the average British import . . . While the film was manufactured in England, Producers Irving Allen and A. R. Broccoli wisely availed themselves of the best filmmaking techniques of that country and their native Hollywood."[8] The Warwick films tended to be solid box-office performers in the United States: their domestic theatrical rentals—for example *Paratrooper* ($1,750,000), *The Black Knight* ($1,700,000), *Hell Below Zero* ($1,700,000), and *Safari* ($1,400,000)—were usually sufficient to place them in the lower half of the top hundred releases of the year.[9]

According to Richard Maibaum, the American screenwriter who wrote the scripts for *The Red Beret*, *The Cockleshell Heroes*, *Zarak*, and *No Time to Die*, Broccoli had first expressed an interest in the James Bond books in the mid-1950s:

> In 1956 or 1957, when I was in England writing for Cubby and Irving Allen, Cubby gave me two of the James Bond books to read. I read them and liked them enormously. Cubby was very excited, but Irving Allen didn't share his enthusiasm. So Cubby put them aside. It's my personal opinion now that that

was a wise thing to do, because with the censorship of pictures that existed then, you couldn't even have the minimal sex and violence that we eventually put into the pictures. They just wouldn't have been the same.[10]

Broccoli confirmed this in his autobiography, placing the episode in 1958, probably around the time of the publication of *Dr. No*. In his account, Broccoli set up a meeting with Fleming and his literary agent at Les Ambassadeurs Club in Mayfair, London, but was unable to attend when he had to fly to New York to attend to his wife Nedra, terminally ill with cancer. Irving Allen, who was notably less enthusiastic than his partner, met Fleming and was reportedly so rude about the quality of his books that the deal went nowhere: "The Fleming contingent were justifiably put out, wondering why they'd bothered to attend the meeting in the first place. So the tenuous link I had with the James Bond books in 1958 was broken. Fortunately, not for ever."[11]

However, by the late 1950s, the changing landscape of the British film industry signaled the end for Warwick. A temporary caesura in the relationship with Columbia Pictures saw Allen and Broccoli set up as independent distributors with Eros Films in 1957. The initiative was not a success, and they soon negotiated a new production/distribution arrangement with the studio.[12] The decline of the regular cinemagoing audience on both sides of the Atlantic squeezed the market for the sort of middle-budget genre films in which Warwick specialized. (Their later films fared less well at the box office.) The company's last film suggested a more culturally ambitious direction: the costume drama *The Trials of Oscar Wilde* (1960), with a budget of £269,546. It was a critical success but lost money at the box office. Broccoli attributed its failure in the United States to the film's boycott by the Catholic Legion of Decency and other religious groups due to its scandalous content; this made major cinema circuits reluctant to book it and limited its release to the art house circuit.[13] At this point, Allen and Broccoli decided to go their separate ways. Allen subsequently produced *The Hellions* (1961) and *The Long Ships* (1964) for Columbia.

Harry Saltzman had a different career trajectory. He was a Canadian who had started out as a theatre and television producer in New York before coming to Europe in the mid-1950s, where he produced the Bob Hope–Katharine Hepburn comedy *The Iron Petticoat* (1956) in Britain and the telefilm series *Captain Gallant of the Foreign Legion* (1956) in Italy. Prior to Bond, Saltzman's main contribution to British cinema was as producer of the early British new wave films *Look Back in Anger* (1959), *The Entertainer* (1960), and *Saturday Night and Sunday Morning* (1960). He went into partnership with playwright John Osborne and stage director Tony Richardson in order to bring Osborne's critically acclaimed plays to the screen. On the face of it, there would have seemed to be little in common between the abrasive, commercially-minded film producer and the "Angry Young Men" of British theatre. However, Osborne felt that Saltzman's largesse—a combination of flattery, promises of untold riches, and the services of high-class French prostitutes—concealed a more sensitive and cultured individual: "He talked fluently, as if we had grown up together, with a familiarity that was neither intrusive nor objectionable. In spite of massive presumptions, he also had an instinct for reticence." Osborne said that it was Saltzman who "wanted to make films of *Look Back* and *The Entertainer*."[14] Tony Richardson also expressed a curious kind of affection for Saltzman: "He was—though the word wasn't in vogue then—a hustler, but a sublime hustler. And I don't mean the word pejoratively."[15]

It has become part of the orthodoxy of British cinema history that no distributor wanted to back the film of *Look Back in Anger*. However, the adaptation of successful theatrical and literary properties was a tried-and-tested strategy for British filmmakers. In fact, producers John and James Woolf had approached Osborne with a view to buying the film rights shortly after the play's first run at the Royal Court Theatre in 1956.[16] Osborne declined their offer, as he was keen that Richardson should also direct the film adaptation. The Woolfs turned instead to John Braine's novel *Room at the Top*. *Look Back in Anger* ended up being made by Woodfall Film Productions (set up by Saltzman, Osborne and Richardson) for the Associated British Picture Corporation (ABPC). Associated British was the smaller of the two such vertically integrated corporations in Britain, the larger being the Rank Organization, and was generally regarded as being an economically and culturally conservative outfit disinclined to take risks. Its decision to back *Look Back in Anger* was determined in some measure by the fact that Warner Bros., which held a 37.5 percent stake in Associated British, had Richard Burton on a "pay or play" deal and were going to have to pay out £125,000 whether he made a film for them or not. *Look Back in Anger* was a critical success but a commercial failure. Saltzman later told Alexander Walker: "It didn't do much business anywhere in the world. I never made a film that got such good reviews and was seen by so few people."[17]

Woodfall's next two films were backed by independent British distributor Bryanston Films, which advanced 70 percent of the budget; the balance was provided by loans from the National Film Finance Corporation (NFFC) and through producer deferments. The NFFC had been set up in 1949 in response to a financial crisis in the British film industry: it provided "end money" loans—the part of the budget not covered by standard distribution contracts—for independent producers. *The Entertainer*, which starred Laurence Olivier as washed-up music hall comedian Archie Rice, was another loss-maker, returning UK distributor's receipts of only £79,935 (including £22,582 from the Eady levy) against a production cost of £205,129.[18] By contrast, *Saturday Night and Sunday Morning*, directed by Karel Reisz and adapted by Alan Sillitoe from his own novel at a modest cost of £120,604, returned UK distributor's receipts of £555,264 (including an Eady payment of £155,511).[19] The one party who did not benefit financially from *Saturday Night and Sunday Morning* was Saltzman, whose share of the profits was assigned to the ABPC.[20]

Saltzman was an intellectually restless producer, always looking for the next popular trend. He cut his ties with Woodfall following *Saturday Night and Sunday Morning*, suggesting that he thought the new wave had run its course: "All the films were designed to show how the other half lives, but for God's sake, we *are* the other half! I thought it was time to go back to big entertainment and I saw in the Bonds the bigger than life thing."[21] Saltzman acquired a six-month option on the entire

Bond series except *Casino Royale* from Fleming in late 1960.[22] On the face of it, he had chosen his moment well. James Bond's popularity was on the rise at the time. The total UK paperback sales of the books doubled from 323,000 in 1960 to 670,000 in 1961.[23] *Thunderball*, the ninth Bond title, was published on March 27, 1961 and quickly sold out its first print run of fifty thousand copies. Earlier that month, *Life* magazine published an article in which *From Russia, with Love* was named as one of John F. Kennedy's favorite books. Andrew Lycett suggests that the US president's reading matter—titles dominated by political biographies, but that also included Stendahl's *The Scarlet and the Black* and Peter Quennell's *Byron in Italy*—was "an eclectic list designed to show that Kennedy was both well-read and in tune with popular taste."[24] The presidential endorsement was a welcome fillip that no doubt helped to raise public awareness of Bond in the United States.

However, Saltzman was unable to secure the finances to produce the films. He even had to borrow money to extend his option. Film Finances had provided the guarantee of completion for both *The Entertainer* and *Saturday Night and Sunday Morning*. Its archive includes a letter of agreement dated June 19, 1961 whereby a Film Finance acquisition, Edward Dryhurst Productions, made Saltzman an interest-free loan of £6,500 secured against his share of the profits in *Saturday Night and Sunday Morning*.[25] The loan was arranged through Saltzman's London solicitor, Brian Lewis, a founder of the law firm Harbottle & Lewis, which also represented Film Finances. The purpose of the loan is not stated in the agreement, but the timing makes it at least a possibility that it was connected to Saltzman's renewing his soon-to-expire option on the Bond books. Furthermore, the date of the agreement was immediately before Saltzman accompanied Broccoli to meet the United Artists board in New York. It is entirely plausible that Film Finances made the loan with a tacit understanding that Saltzman would bring the business to them for a completion guarantee. An internal note by managing director Robert Garrett in the Film Finances Archive *Dr. No* file dated July 4, 1961 records that UA's European division head "[George] Ornstein informed me today that they had made a deal with Brockley [*sic*] & Saltzman for the Bond picture and that they will be coming to us for a Guarantee."[26] The loan was repaid on Saltzman's behalf by Bryanston Films in several installments between November 8, 1961 and April 6, 1962.[27]

The partnership between Saltzman and Broccoli—who were introduced by their mutual friend Wolf Mankowitz—was essentially a marriage of convenience: one man held the option on the Bond books and the other had the connections with the moneymen. Broccoli felt obliged to offer Columbia Pictures first refusal on the Bond pictures given his long-standing association with the studio. In hindsight, its decision to pass seems as fateful as Decca's rejection of The Beatles a few months later. However, the studio's most successful British productions in the late 1950s and early 1960s had been war and historical epics— *The Bridge on the River Kwai* (1957), *The Guns of Navarone* (1961), and *Lawrence of Arabia* (1962)—whereas the Bond books were regarded as lowbrow thrillers suitable only for "B" movies. In one account, Broccoli averred that Columbia had offered a budget of between $300,000 and $400,000 for either *Dr. No* or *Thunderball*.[28]

In any event, it was United Artists that agreed to finance and distribute the Bond films. Broccoli's memoirs offer this account of his and Saltzman's meeting with UA chairman Arthur Krim and his board:

> We flew to New York, me with Dana, Harry with his wife Jacqui. At the appointed hour, Harry and I entered Arthur Krim's office. I wasn't prepared for the battalion of executives he'd assembled for the discussions. With Krim were his partner Bob Benjamin, David Picker and all the publicity chiefs: clearly they felt they were on to something big. They spoke in awesome terms about sums approaching $1 million. (Twenty years later they'd be casually mentioning billions.) With all that top brass on show, I felt excited. Churning away in my mind was the absolute conviction that James Bond was going to be a revelation in motion pictures. We had some argument about the music rights: no small item in the logistics of film-making, for many a movie has produced gold discs from its soundtrack... The budget was agreed at $1 million. Our share of the profits—after they had recovered their investment—would be sixty per cent for us, forty per cent for them. We all shook hands. We had a deal. It had taken no more than thirty-five or forty minutes.[29]

Broccoli recounts that he and Saltzman left the meeting with a verbal agreement but nothing in writing. It would take until

April 1962—after *Dr. No* had completed shooting—for the financing and distribution agreements for the series to be formalized.[30] The first report in the film trade press appeared in *Boxoffice* on July 3, 1961: "[UA] has just closed a production deal with producers Cubby Broccoli and Harry Saltzman, calling for the financing and distribution of a series of pictures based on the best-selling novels by Ian Fleming . . . The first picture will be either *Dr. No* or *Diamonds Are Forever*."[31]

Most other accounts suggest that *Thunderball* was to have been the first Bond picture. There are different explanations as to why *Dr. No* was preferred instead. Broccoli attributed it to the lawsuit brought against Fleming in the High Court in London by producer Kevin McClory and screenwriter Jack Whittingham, who averred that the author was in breach of copyright as he had used plot elements from an unrealized Bond film script in *Thunderball*. Broccoli's memoirs state: "We had originally planned *Thunderball* as the first Bond film. In fact, we had Dick Maibaum write the script. But the day Dick completed it, Kevin McClory brought his injunction against Ian Fleming. United Artists were nervous about getting into a film with a controversy hanging over it, and rejected it."[32] This account is not correct in the details: Maibaum's *Thunderball* script is dated August 18, 1961, whereas McClory and Whittingham's writ against Fleming was issued five months earlier, on March 21.[33] However, UA's David Picker suggested that the preference for *Dr. No* came down to cost: "They suggested *Thunderball*, but having read the book I felt the story was going to be too expensive to shoot as the first picture. *Dr. No* lent itself better to the guidelines we set."[34]

United Artists' support for the Bond pictures should be seen as part of the corporation's economic and cultural investment in British production during the 1960s. UA differed from the other Hollywood majors insofar as it did not own its own studio facilities and was therefore reliant upon independent producers for all its output. This also meant that it was particularly well placed to adjust to the decline of the studio system and the rise of runaway production. UA had a long-standing presence in Britain, where it had backed major independent producers such as Alexander Korda and Herbert Wilcox in the 1930s. Tino Balio avers that UA's British production program "consisted of a diversified range of product suitable for all markets."[35] In the early 1960s, its British films included several residual genres, notably the war film, exemplified by *The Valiant* (1962) and *633 Squadron* (1964), and comedies such as *The Mouse on the Moon* (1963) and *A Shot in the Dark* (1964). But UA was also quick to recognize the emergence of a new trend in British cinema for films that reflected the changing social politics and sexual mores of the decade. As well as the Bond pictures, it backed *Tom Jones* (1963)—a bawdy adaptation of Henry Fielding's eighteenth-century romp produced by Woodfall Films—and the Beatles musicals *A Hard Day's Night* (1964) and *Help!* (1965). UA financed *Tom Jones* when Bryanston balked at the £420,000 budget. UA was popular with independent producers because it offered a higher share of the profits—typically a fifty–fifty division between producer and distributor—and was less interventionist than other studios. According to David Picker: "Once approvals on any project were given, the production was on its own with no involvement from UA in any way. Occasionally I might visit a location as a courtesy, or be invited to see dailies, but basically the producers were on their own ... We had nobody on the set watching any of the day-to-day trials and tribulations that occur on any film."[36]

The Film Finances Archive holds copies of the financing and distribution contracts for *Dr. No* and the subsequent films. These make it abundantly clear that a series was planned from the outset. According to the April 10, 1962 financing agreement between Danjaq and United Artists, the producer

> has agreed to cause to be produced, completed and delivered to United one (1) or more additional new and original feature length sound and talking motion picture photoplays in the English language based upon the so-called "James Bond Stories" written by said Ian Fleming, some of which are entitled *Live and Let Die, Moonraker, Thunderball, From Russia With Love, Goldfinger, Casino Royale, For Your Eyes Only* and *Diamonds Are Forever.*

The contract went on to clarify that the producers warranted they had secured options from Fleming to produce "one or more feature length motion picture photoplays based upon or related to each book," including future books, with the exceptions of *Casino Royale* ("the motion picture rights to which have heretofore been assigned to the late Gregory Ratoff") and *Thunderball* ("the screenplay rights to which are presently subject to litigation"). *Thunderball* was to be included in the agreement "when, as and if the Producer acquires a clear legal title to the motion picture rights with respect thereto."[37] The *Thunderball* case was finally resolved in November 1963: Kevin McClory was assigned the film rights in that novel alone.[38]

The financing agreement laid out the basis on which the early Bond pictures would be produced. United Artists would advance 100 percent of the agreed budget in return for worldwide distribution rights. The actual production loan would be made by the London branch of the Bank of America. The producers would pay Fleming $100,000 per film, the option fee to be charged to the budget. UA exercised the right of approval of title, writer, director, script, principal cast, budget, and schedule. It could require the producer to option a particular book and "in the event of disagreement between United and the Producer as to which Book to select, United shall have the right to make the final determination." A peculiar condition of the agreement was that "each Picture shall be photographed in black and white unless United shall approve photography of said Picture in colour"; the same clause included UA's approval for *Dr. No* to be shot in Technicolor. A further condition was that the producer would secure a guarantee of completion from Film Finances. Following deduction of the distributor's fees and expenses and repayment of the production loan, the net profits for each film would be shared equally between UA and the producers. Fleming was to be paid 5 percent of the profits of each film, "which shall be borne equally by United and Producer out of their respective shares of the net profits of such Picture." (Broccoli's account that the producers' share was originally 60 percent of the profits is therefore incorrect. However, the financing agreement included a provision that if the first two films recovered their costs, the producers' share would increase to 60 percent with the third film.)

The distribution agreement between Danjaq and United Artists included further clauses that had an important bearing on the production of the Bond films. *Dr. No* was "to be capable of being duly registered as a British film and as an Exhibitor's Quota film and of participating in the British Film Production Fund as an eligible film."[39] The significance attached to the Eady levy suggests that UA expected the film to have particular box-office appeal in the British market. To this extent, the production ecology of the Bond films would be very similar to that of Warwick Films: Eon Productions was a British-registered company that would undertake the actual production of the films. A clause entitled "Producer's Negative Covenant on Television" stipulated that the author would not participate in a television series for at least five years after the last film option was taken up. The covenant was very probably included due to Fleming's involvement in the origin and early development of the television series that would become *The Man from U.N.C.L.E.* Fleming had worked with producer Norman Felton on the concept of the series for the NBC network: he had suggested the names of the protagonist Napoleon Solo and heroine April Dancer. He pulled out of any further involvement in the series, originally titled *Solo*, in July 1963.[40] The first season of *The Man from U.N.C.L.E.* premiered on NBC in September 1964, a month after Fleming's death.[41]

It has sometimes been suggested that *Dr. No* was a relatively low-budget film. Even Broccoli himself described it as having "a strictly limited production budget."[42] This needs to be placed in context. The first production budget submitted to Film Finances was £317,359.[43] This was somewhere in the upper middle of the budget range for a British first feature in the early 1960s. In 1963, for example, F. L. Thomas, managing director of the British division of Rank Film Distributors, told *Kine Weekly* that the cost of "an averagely good, well-polished, well-starred picture" was £200,000–250,000, though there was the occasional "sleeper" made for £80,000–100,000: "For a truly international picture, one had to think in terms of upwards of £500,000."[44] Other British films backed by United Artists in the early 1960s included *Tunes of Glory* (£271,165), *The Valiant* (£181,000), and *Tom Jones* (£412,374). An internal memo from UA's publicity department stated that "*Dr. No* is a major production. It is in color with a big budget."[45] It received similar funding as *The Ipcress File* (£309,261)—a more realistic spy picture produced by Harry Saltzman independently of Eon in 1965 that would be the first of a trilogy of films adapted from the novels of Len Deighton—but less than other British-made spy films of the mid-1960s, including *Deadlier Than the Male* (£540,683) and *The Quiller Memorandum* (£956,359). The high cost of the latter film was due in large measure to the fees paid to costar Alec Guinness (who received £89,286—the equivalent of US$250,000—for what amounted to a glorified cameo as spymaster Pohl) and scriptwriter Harold Pinter.[46] By contemporary standards, therefore, *Dr. No* was a well-budgeted British feature but was not at the very top end of the budget range.

Broccoli always maintained that his outlook as a producer was to put the budget on the screen: he would rather invest in production values than in salaries or cast. This is borne out by the budget of *Dr. No*. The total "above the line" expenses (script, producer and director fees) amounted to 29.6 percent of the budget. The most expensive category was "story and script," accounting for 15.5 percent. This included Ian Fleming's fee of £35,715 (the sterling equivalent of $100,000) as well as payments to scriptwriters Wolf Mankowitz, Richard Maibaum, Johanna Harwood, and Berkely Mather. Terence Young's fee for directing was £15,000 plus an expense allowance of £2,500, around a par figure for a director at the time. (Young had opted for a higher up-front fee rather than a percentage of the profits.) The cast budget, amounting to only 8.4 percent of the total, was rather lower than average for a major feature film. This reflected the fact that there were no "stars" as such in *Dr. No*. The main cast budget does not identify payments to individuals, but a separate document headed "Dr. No—Estimated Cast Budget" (December 12, 1961) lists the allocation per role: the seven highest-paid were Bond (£6,000), Dr. No (£5,382/$15,000), Felix Leiter (£2,857/$8,000), Honey Rider (£1,500), Professor Dent (£1,500), Quarrel (£750), and Miss Taro (£600). It is likely that the two "foreign" individuals excluded from the statutory costs of the film were Americans Richard Maibaum and Joseph Wiseman (who played Dr. No). Saltzman (a Canadian citizen) and Broccoli (a long-term UK resident) could be included in the British salary costs. After the producers, who each received £7,143, and the director, the highest-paid technicians were production manager L. C. Rudkin (£2,849), production designer Ken Adam (£2,563), production accountant Stanley Sopel (£2,400) and director of photography Ted Moore

(£1,312). The producers' remuneration was low by contemporary standards, but United Artists' records reveal that Saltzman and Broccoli deferred part of their fees and overheads in order to reduce the budget.[47]

The limited cast budget of *Dr. No* sheds some light on the casting decisions. This area has been the subject of a great deal of misinformation. For example, it is sometimes reported that Cary Grant (star of Hitchcock's *North by Northwest*) was considered for the role of Bond. This is extremely unlikely on purely budgetary grounds, let alone the fact that Grant would turn fifty-eight years old at the time of shooting; his fee of $300,000 per picture plus 10 percent of the rental earnings would have priced him out of consideration.[48] There was a good deal of speculation about casting in the press. The *Daily Express* ran a competition to find the public's choice for the "ideal" Bond. The winner was male model Peter Anthony, who won a readers' poll ahead of several others, including stuntman Bob Simmons.[49] The Jamaican *Daily Gleaner*—which took a keen interest in *Dr. No* when it became known that the locations for the film would be shot on the island—reported that Saltzman said he planned to test Patrick Allen and that "I'm also thinking about Michael Craig and Patrick McGoohan, but I'd prefer to use an unknown."[50] Broccoli also averred that McGoohan—at the time starring as secret agent John Drake in the British-made telefilm series *Danger Man*—was under consideration. So, supposedly, were James Fox, Roger Moore, David Niven, and Trevor Howard, while Terence Young is reported to have preferred Richard Johnson.[51] McGoohan was perhaps the most plausible of these possible Bond candidates: he looked the part and was the right age (34). However, it is widely held that his strong religious beliefs and his aversion to sex and violence on screen ruled him out of contention. Roger Moore would later play Bond—he starred in seven films from *Live and Let Die* (1973) to *A View to a Kill* (1985)—though at the time of *Dr. No* he was committed to the television series *The Saint*. It is quite possible that his frequent inclusion on the list of Bond contenders in 1961 is a form of retrospective validation of his later casting.

United Artists' records reveal that another actor not mentioned in any of the published accounts did receive serious consideration. On September 18, 1961, Ornstein wrote to Picker:

> Further to your telegram I arranged a screening of *The Valiant* for Cubby Broccoli and Harry Saltzman, and I must say the actor Robert Shaw in this particular film did not impress any of us as being James Bond. However, this may be entirely due to the fact that he was always in uniform and, with the exception of one or two scenes, wearing his cap and when not wearing it, his hair was very tussled [*sic*]. I talked with Broccoli and Saltzman and we are going to locate other pictures that Robert Shaw played in before being able to give you a definite opinion.[52]

At the time, Shaw was best known for the swashbuckling adventure series *The Buccaneers* (1956–1957), produced in Britain by the Independent Television Programme Company and aired by the CBS network in the United States. While the actor was not deemed appropriate for Bond, he would be cast as assassin Red Grant in *From Russia with Love*.

The role of Bond went to thirty-one-year-old Sean Connery, whose casting was announced in early November 1961.[53] Several points need to be made in relation to Connery's casting. The first is that he was very far from being an unknown actor: Connery already had a substantial body of work on television—including BBC studio dramas of *Requiem for a Heavyweight* and *Anna Karenina* (in which he co-starred opposite Claire Bloom on the day his casting as Bond was announced)—as well as supporting roles in a number of films, including *Another Time, Another Place* (1958) and *The Frightened City* (1961). Broccoli's account that he was persuaded to cast Connery after seeing him in the Disney fantasy *Darby O'Gill and the Little People* (1959) is confirmed by the Film Finances Archive: the first item charged to the budget of *Dr. No* was a screening fee ($23.63) for that picture at the Goldwyn Studios (UA's Hollywood base) in Los Angeles on June 28, 1961. Contrary to accounts that he initially felt Connery was too rough around the edges and only warmed to him after meeting the actor on location in Jamaica, Ian Fleming approved of the choice. On October 25, 1961, Fleming wrote to his confidante Blanche Blackwell: "The producer [*sic*], Terence Young, seems very nice and the man they have chosen for Bond, Sean Connery, is a real charmer—fairly unknown but a good actor with the right looks and physique."[54]

David Picker stated that the choice of director for *Dr. No* was between Terence Young and Guy Hamilton. Broccoli suggested that Guy Green and Ken Hughes were also approached but declined.⁵⁵ Tino Balio claims that the producers initially favored American director Phil Karlson, but his agent wanted too much money. Broccoli's memoir does not mention Karlson. An American director would probably have affected the film's eligibility for the Eady levy.⁵⁶ Young had directed four films for Warwick—*The Red Beret*, *Safari*, *Zarak*, and *No Time to Die*—as well as a similar action picture for MGM, *Action of the Tiger* (1957), which had featured Sean Connery in a bit part. However, he had a reputation for going over budget. Film Finances, which provided the completion guarantee for *Action of the Tiger*, felt that "this script is a typical example of the sort of thing over which he has gone sadly wrong in the past. It is full of action—which we know is not Mr. Young's strong point, either from a directorial point of view or for speed of shooting."⁵⁷ Picker felt that the choice of Young was largely to do with the director's bon vivant lifestyle, noting: "As a matter of fact, had he been some years younger, *he* could have played James Bond . . . Terence dressed from Savile Row. Terence ate at Les Ambassadeurs, the poshest place in London."⁵⁸ Young—admittedly not the most reliable source—claimed that Ian Fleming's first comment to him was: "So they've decided on you to fuck up my work."⁵⁹

In mid-December 1961, a month before shooting was due to commence in Jamaica, Eon Productions submitted the paperwork for *Dr. No*, including the budget, script, and schedule, to Film Finances for a completion guarantee as required by the financing agreement with United Artists. Saltzman told UA: "I believe that we will have a rough time convincing Film Finances to accept this budget [£317,359] but at most we may be forced to increase four or five thousand pounds in order to satisfy them."⁶⁰ Saltzman and Broccoli were both well known to Film Finances, which had guaranteed *The Iron Petticoat*, *The Entertainer, Saturday Night and Sunday Morning*, and nine of Warwick's films. Both producers had a not-undeserved reputation for profligacy, though it was Terence Young who was the main cause of concern for production consultant John Croydon in his assessment of the proposition:

> I had liked the script and the look of these papers until I heard that Terence Young was to be the director!
>
> The script is dealt with in master scenes, [and] is a very good interpretation, I thought, of the Ian Fleming book and does not present too much in the way of production hazard. It is crisp in its approach, not too long and altogether, a very workmanlike job.
>
> The schedule did not give me any apprehension. There are one or two places where it is essential the director states his intentions, such as the chase from the Airport, culminating in the murder and especially the scenes where Bond first gets to the island, including the swamp scenes. There is no reason why, once the producer has fixed a period in which these sequences should be shot, they should not be achieved. However, it is when one has to consider what Terence Young is likely to do with them, that trepidation in expressing opinions, comes into play.
>
> So far as the studio is concerned, the items which need our especial attention are—Dr. No's Apartment with the BP [back projection] representation of the bed of the ocean; the re-actor [*sic*] room and the method to be employed to obtain

the effect of Dr. No's "scissor" hands. None of these items ought to cause bother; they are simple effects, if approached from the point of view of simplicity. I only hope that Terence Young doesn't want to be "clever" over any or all of them![61]

Croydon proceeded to list a number of specific areas where he felt the film was underbudgeted. He was concerned that the budget did not include any allowance for Sunday working (expensive due to overtime payments); the allowance for makeup and hairdressing was on the low side; at only £1,190, music "seemed to be under-budgeted"; and the publicity budget (£1,156) "seems very low for a Saltzman picture."

Croydon's assessment of the proposition provides some revealing insights into the personalities and reputations of the people involved. As associate producer on a previous picture, he was aware of Saltzman's habit of running up high long-distance bills ("I wondered about the charge of £1,000 for telephone calls, bearing in mind the size of Saltzman's bills on *The Entertainer*!") and he was wary of the director's reputation for shooting excess footage ("120,000 > of Eastman neg. seemed enough for the job, though I think Young eats it for breakfast!!"). The estimated costume costs "seem to lie in an 'in between' category. If no 'House' was to be employed to dress the women, then the figure seemed high, but if 'creations' were expected, the amount did not seem enough. We must remember the propensity of Saltzman and Young to go rushing off to the Paris 'houses' in such circumstances!" Croydon concluded "that under normal conditions the schedule could be accepted . . . but I must confess to some alarm at the combination of Broccoli, Saltzman, and

Young in charge of the picture, especially as Rudkin, although a good PM [production manager], is probably not the strongest controller of people of this type." However, he recommended that Film Finances accept the proposition.

Film Finances issued its letter of intent—an agreement in principle to guarantee the completion of the film subject to oversight of the distribution and studio contracts, a letter from the director confirming that the schedule and allocation of film stock were sufficient, and an undertaking from the producers to "cast to budget"—on December 18, 1961. The letter of intent stipulated that the budget would be £321,227, an increase of £3,868 over the original production budget to address the areas where the film was deemed to be underbudgeted. Additional conditions beyond the usual terms of the guarantee addressed specific concerns in Croydon's report: that the production designer (Ken Adam) would provide a letter confirming that the budget for set construction was adequate, that the producers would confirm that the budget allowance for music was adequate, and that any publicity expenditure above the budgeted allowance would be met by the distributor rather than charged to the film. It also required confirmation that the £9,750 cost of a charter aircraft to transport cast and crew to and from Jamaica was "an inclusive deal."[62] However, the letter of intent did not mention a separate arrangement whereby Terence Young had agreed to place £10,000 of his salary in escrow as a protection against any overspending incurred through his own extravagance.[63] This would later be the cause of some grievance on Young's part. Further small adjustments prior to the commencement of photography would increase the budget to £322,069.[64]

Chapter Three

MONKEY BUSINESS

ONE OF THE MOST persistent myths about the first Bond film is that an early draft of the script had Dr. No as a monkey. This is another of those oft-repeated stories whose origin has become obscured. It was lent some weight by Cubby Broccoli's memoir, where he claimed that writers Richard Maibaum and Wolf Mankowitz provided a treatment in which "they had decided to make Dr No a monkey. I repeat: a monkey." Broccoli (or possibly his collaborator Donald Zec) embellishes the story thus: "This threw Harry and me into some dismay. A million dollars was being invested in bringing James Bond to the screen. We didn't think that a monkey, even with a high IQ, could in any circumstances be 007's 'merciless antagonist' . . . Also, Harry and I didn't think United Artists would take kindly to the notion of Britain's most feared secret agent pitting himself against a spider monkey, however ingenious the plot."[1] However, the suggestion that Dr. No was a monkey, let alone an intelligent one, in any script or treatment is simply not correct: its persistence is yet another case of an anecdote being repeated so often that it becomes accepted as fact. Indeed, much of what has been written about the scripting of *Dr. No* is based on a mixture of unreliable testimony and half-truths.

It is widely acknowledged in the film industry that script credits often conceal as much as they reveal about the actual creative inputs into a film: *Dr. No* is no exception. The credit on the film's opening titles ("Screenplay by Richard Maibaum, Johanna Harwood, Berkely Mather") does not necessarily mean that all those named made an equal contribution or even that they were the only writers involved. As so often happens, the anecdotal sources are contradictory. Richard Maibaum, for example, gave the following account of the scripting process in an interview with Pat McGilligan:

> *Thunderball* was actually the first, we decided it was the one to start with. I finished a first draft, and then Kevin McClory jumped up with a lawsuit against Ian Fleming, claiming that he wrote the novel after they'd done a screen treatment together. So we put *Thunderball* aside until that was settled and decided to do *Dr. No*. I was then in London, after having finished the first draft of *Thunderball*, so I began to write *Dr. No* with Wolf Mankowitz. Cubby and Harry didn't like our first treatment, so Wolf bowed out, and I went on to do the first draft of the screenplay. Later, after I left, a novelist named Aubrey [*sic*] Mather (Jasper Davis is his real name) did some work on it with a girl playwright, Joanna [*sic*] Harwood.[2]

Terence Young gave a different account that omits Mather's contribution while suggesting that he and Harwood knocked the script into shape. He told Richard Schenkman:

> We had at one time, I think, five different scripts on *Dr No* including one in which Dr No was a monkey. It was the craziest thing... That's how this girl, Joanna [*sic*] Harwood, who was my continuity girl on a previous picture, got in it with me. We took a room at the Dorchester Hotel, and we worked day and night. I used to give her things to write, like I'd say, "James Bond comes out of this, gets in the car, and drives off. Just put it in, wearing this...," and I'd go on writing another scene with dialogue. She did that and she did it very well.[3]

And Johanna Harwood's account, as recounted to Matthew Field, was that she was working for Harry Saltzman as a script editor at the time he acquired his option on the Bond books:

> I came in at the start. I'd written several screenplays for Saltzman by this time, of course, none of which he'd made, but I'd done a good few. He asked me to do a short synopsis of each book—I think five or six of them were out—and he went over to America to do the deal... We were aiming to make a proper spy story and we'd sit around having script conferences, discussing Bond's psychological motivations. Nobody thought it would turn out to be comic.[4]

Harwood claimed to have written a draft of *Dr. No* before other writers became involved: "Wolf Mankowitz and Richard

Maibaum were sent off to the country to a hotel for about a month. And they re-wrote the script. And when they brought it back—you're never going to believe this—Dr No turned out to be an intelligent monkey!"[5]

Where anecdotal sources are at variance, the archival record may provide some answers. The production budget for *Dr. No* held by the Film Finances Archive lists payments to four writers: Wolf Mankowitz (£7,000), Richard Maibaum (£5,100), Johanna Harwood (£300) and Berkely Mather (£1,000).[6] This would suggest *prima facie* that Mankowitz and Maibaum both made more substantial contributions than either Harwood or Mather. The fact that Harwood was paid significantly less than the other writers is noteworthy. It might reflect a gendered pay difference (this would be consistent with other aspects of the budgeting of *Dr. No*: the "wardrobe master" was budgeted at £35 per week compared to £25 per week for the "wardrobe mistress"), or it may simply be that Harwood did have a lesser input than the others. If Harwood did indeed write a treatment, or even a full script of *Dr. No*, this would surely have been compensated at more than £300. It may be that Harry Saltzman paid for this work from his own pocket, though at the same time it also seems unlikely that the cash-strapped producer would not have charged this to the budget as a development cost.

The first contemporary report of the scripting of *Dr. No* in the trade press was a short notice in *Kine Weekly* at the end of July 1961: "The prolific pen of Wolf Mankowitz has been signed by Harry Saltzman and 'Cubby' Broccoli to do the screenplay of *Dr. No*, first of the James Bond series which the producers are making for United Artists."[7] Mankowitz was a British playwright and novelist who became involved in the film industry when he adapted his own novel *A Kid for Two Farthings*—a semiautobiographical account of his childhood in the Jewish community of London's East End—for the film directed by Carol Reed in 1956. This led to other scriptwriting commissions, including the pop music satire *Expresso Bongo* (1959), based on his own play, the Hammer horror *Two Faces of Dr. Jekyll* (1960), the Peter Sellers–Sophia Loren comedy *The Millionairess* (1960), and the apocalyptic science-fiction drama *The Day the Earth Caught Fire* (1961). Mankowitz's £7,000 fee suggests that his input must have been significant, though the anecdotal sources suggest that it came early in the process and that he was not involved in later drafts. It seems to be accepted that the omission of Mankowitz's name from the finished film was at his own request. An oft-quoted anecdote is that he told the producers: "I don't like it at all. I think it's a load of crap . . . It's so bad that I don't want anything to do with it."[8]

Mankowitz worked with American screenwriter Richard Maibaum on the early drafts. Maibaum represents a link between the Bond pictures and the era of classical Hollywood. He had been one of a group of progressive playwrights in New York during the 1930s who were recruited by Hollywood. (The others included Elia Kazan, John Huston, and Robert Rossen.) He was employed at various studios, including MGM, Columbia, and Paramount. After the Second World War, Maibaum worked as a writer and occasional producer—he produced the television series of *The Thin Man* for MGM in the late 1950s— and wrote several scripts for Warwick Film Productions, including *The Red Beret* (1953), *Hell Below Zero* (1954), *The Cockleshell*

Heroes (1955), *Zarak* (1956), and *No Time to Die* (1958). Maibaum's previous association with both Broccoli and Terence Young made him a natural choice for *Dr. No*. He would go on to receive script credits on thirteen Bond pictures, the last being *Licence to Kill* (1989). Adrian Turner suggests that he had significant cultural agency in the development of the Bond films, writing: "Maibaum must be regarded as a key contributor to the Bond ethos and the Bond machine: its creation surely owes nearly as much to him as it does to Ian Fleming, or to Saltzman and Broccoli, or to Sean Connery and Ken Adam."[9]

Maibaum believed that the popular appeal of the films was rooted in Fleming's books. In an article for the *New York Times* in 1964, he wrote: "There is little doubt in my mind that the success of the Bond films stem directly from the success of the novels, their combination of terror and elegance, sophistication and suspense, the unabashed but beautifully depicted episodes, the projection of James Bond's character as an escape image with which millions delightfully identify themselves."[10] Maibaum went on to explain that there were certain aspects of Fleming's books that did not transfer easily onto the screen, especially his descriptive prose and the stream-of-consciousness passages featuring insights into Bond's thinking. Nevertheless, Maibaum's scripts would often transpose Fleming's descriptions of characters' appearance and even chunks of dialogue. His thirteen Bond credits include twelve where he is credited with another writer and just one—*On Her Majesty's Secret Service* (1969)—where he is the sole writer: this was also the closest of the films to Fleming's book. Maibaum's first screenplay of *Thunderball* (August 18, 1961), written before he began working on

Dr. No and for which he is the sole credited writer, is also very close to the source text.[11] Maibaum reflected: "Unlike *Thunderball*, *Dr. No* was a monster to lick, especially under the modus operandi which began to evolve during the preparation of the screenplay: the US method ... After I write and submit my first draft of the screenplay, revisions are discussed in committee. Put baldly this is essentially a group attempt to hammer out a final shooting script."[12]

The development of *Dr. No* can be traced through the various script drafts held by the University of Iowa and the British Film Institute. All the drafts from the first treatment (September 7, 1961) to the "Fourth Draft Screenplay" (December 12, 1961) bear the names of Maibaum and Mankowitz. The scripting process was somewhat unusual insofar as it gradually brought the film closer to the book rather than vice versa: most novel-into-film adaptations become more distant from the source text as they progress, but it was the other way around with *Dr. No*. The first treatment is a descriptive scene breakdown of some forty-two pages that is especially notable for its difference in both structure and detail from Fleming's book.[13] While maintaining some scenes from the novel, including the opening in which the three blind beggars assassinate Strangways, Bond's reequipping with a new gun, and the tropical centipede in Bond's bed, the September 7 treatment otherwise makes significant changes from the source text. Bond meets Honey much earlier than in the book; Felix Leiter of the CIA, a character in other Bond novels but not *Dr. No*, is written into the story; Quarrel's role is reduced to little more than a boatman; Pus-Feller becomes one of Dr. No's operatives; and a secondary villain is introduced in the form of Gomez, a Cuban exile who turns out to be procuring arms for pro-Castro groups in Latin America. In this treatment, Dr. No is the head of a Chinese secret society known as the Black Monkey Tong and his guano plant is a cover for arms smuggling. He is described as being six and a half feet tall with claws for hands.

The anecdote that Dr. No was a monkey probably arises from Broccoli and others misremembering this treatment. The symbol of the Black Monkey Tong is "an enormous statue of a Capuchin monkey" that Bond sees in a graveyard on Crab Key: Honey remarks that it must mark the grave of an important man. Shortly afterward, Bond meets Dr. No and realizes that he is an imposter: the clue is a pet Capuchin monkey that he recognizes as one he has previously seen at the home of an English-Creole shipping merchant named Hugh Buckfield who was one of Strangways's bridge partners. Buckfield has assumed the identity of Dr. No—it is implied though not stated explicitly that he killed him—and now controls the Black Monkey Tong ("After the death of my old friend and master, whose grave you had the decency to visit this evening, it was necessary for me to preserve the myth of his invulnerability."). Buckfield plans to load a Cuban-flagged cargo ship with explosives in order to blow up the locks of the Panama Canal. His aim is to provoke American retaliation against Cuba, which will create "a highly-desirable state of chaos in which a resolute and efficient organization like the Black Monkey should become the dominant factor in the Caribbean." Bond and Leiter overcome Buckfield, who perishes in an explosion. The final shot is a close-up of the monkey, Li Ying, and its "gibbering ironic laughter as we FADE OUT and END."

Maibaum and Mankowitz delivered a revised treatment on September 25, 1961: this maintains the basic structure of the first but makes some important changes in detail.[14] Dr. No becomes the primary villain and the description is closer to the character from the book: "He is six and a half feet high, in his early fifties, sinewy and powerful beneath his well-cut Chinese robe. His enormous head is shaven to the skull, his face tear-shaped, tapering down to a smallish chin." He has mechanical hands rather than claws. Buckfield is now Dr. No's lieutenant, an intermediary through whom the villain supplies arms to Gomez. Dr. No kills Buckfield for failing to eliminate Bond by lowering him into a shark tank before Bond's eyes. However, the most important change is to Dr. No's political allegiance. All references to the Black Monkey Tong are removed. Dr. No is described as "not an independent operator but a Red Chinese agent." The People's Republic of China is now behind the plot to blow up the Panama Canal in order to create geopolitical instability in the region. The script explains: "The destruction of the Gatun Locks of the Panama Canal will undoubtedly evoke reprisals by the United States against Cuba. This in turn will prompt Russian action against the United States. Such a situation is considered desirable by Red China ... DR. NO's activities will exploit these conditions both for Red China's benefit and his own."

Klaus Dodds has argued that these early treatments of *Dr. No* demonstrate a conscious realignment of the geopolitics of the book.¹⁵ The inclusion of Leiter, the threat to the Panama Canal, and the references to Cuba all serve to reorient the plot toward the United States. The prominence of Cuba in these early treatments can no doubt be explained insofar as they were written shortly after the Bay of Pigs invasion of April 1961, a failed coup d'état by anti-Castro rebels backed by the CIA. Cuba was a particular concern for newly elected US president John F. Kennedy, who was keen to topple the Castro regime: he had even discussed how this might be done at a dinner with Ian Fleming in March 1960 before his nomination as the Democratic presidential candidate.¹⁶ The threat to blow up the Panama Canal had been used in serials and B movies on the eve of the Second World War—Republic's *Dick Tracy's G-Men* (1939) and Twentieth Century-Fox's *Charlie Chan in Panama* (1940) both featured agents of unnamed foreign powers attempting to do just that—though Dodds suggests that it reflected real geopolitical anxieties in that "as early as the 1950s, American strategic planners were worried that left-wing subversives (supported either by Cuba or the Soviet Union) might seek to disrupt American and Western commercial traffic through an attack on the canal itself."¹⁷ And the shift in Dr. No's allegiance from a freelance criminal associated with an underworld diaspora to an agent of the Chinese state had the effect of "territorializing" the conspiracy: China had hitherto been regarded as an adjunct of the Soviet Union, but by the early 1960s it was clear that the Chinese Communist Party was pursuing its own direction independently of Moscow, including the development of an atomic bomb.¹⁸

The first full screenplay of *Dr. No* is dated October 3, 1961. It is essentially an expanded version of the revised treatment.¹⁹

Dr. No makes an early appearance when Mary Trueblood is kidnapped and taken before him in a ruined fortress; he is seen in silhouette and now has metal pincers for hands. Honey is described as an "incredibly beautiful YOUNG EURASIAN GIRL, half-white, half-Chinese"; in this version, she is one of a group of girls used by Pus-Feller to dive for shells. The conspiracy still has Dr. No supplying arms through Buckfield to Gomez and plotting to blow up the Panama Canal at the behest of Red China ("Dr. No's orders are not subject to Cuban compliance. They implement the policy of the Chinese People's Republic"). Quarrel is absent. Leiter accompanies Bond and Honey on the nighttime canoe expedition to Crab Key; he is presumed dead in the encounter with the motor launch, but turns out to have escaped and facilitates the escape from Dr. No's headquarters in the marsh buggy. Dr. No's cover operation is no longer guano, but rather a bauxite mine. (This mineral with a high aluminum content had become Jamaica's major export commodity by the early 1960s.) However, there is evidence that United Artists was not happy with the direction the script was taking. On October 6, George Ornstein wrote to David Picker: "I must tell you that personally, I have not been impressed to date with Maibaum's work and only hope that he will come up with something much better this time as we have had many story conferences with him."[20]

The script underwent extensive revision and rewriting in late 1961. It is not entirely clear at what point Mankowitz ceased to be involved, though his name continued to be included on all drafts. The "Fourth Draft Screenplay" (December 12, 1961) is much closer to Fleming's novel than the earlier treatments.[21] It has the same basic structure as the book: Bond now meets Honey on Crab Key as originally, Quarrel is restored to a key role, Leiter is not involved in the expedition to Crab Key, and Quarrel is killed in the battle with the marsh buggy. Honey now has her own personal grudge against Dr. No, whom she blames for the death of her marine zoologist father. The characters of Gomez and Buckfield have been combined into a geologist called Professor Dent. The role of Miss Taro, Dr. No's spy inside Government House, is expanded to provide another sexual encounter for Bond: she sets a trap by inviting him to her house while a hearse ambushes him on the road. The centipede in Bond's bed has now become a tarantula, perhaps because the spider was considered more frightening visually. However, the major change from previous drafts is that references to Red China have been dropped and Dr. No has become a member of the international criminal syndicate known as SPECTRE:

BOND

With your sort of disregard for human life you can only be working for the East.

DR. NO (*contemptuously*)

East? West? Points of the compass, Mr. Bond. Each as brutishly stupid as the other. *I* work for SPECTRE.

BOND

Spectre? Never heard of them . . . and I thought I knew all the nuts.

DR. NO
Special Executive for Counter-Intelligence, Terrorism, Revenge and Extortion.

BOND
They sound a pleasant bunch.

(*He looks round and shrugs.*)

Albeit a little theatrical . . . if this is their headquarters.

DR. NO
Headquarters? Don't talk like a fool, Bond. Or are you trying to make me lose my temper? No, this is not their headquarters. Crab Key is but a microcosm of the organisation, syndicate, call it what you will. Do you think that the diversion of a few miserable rockets is the be-all and end-all of our efforts?

BOND (*looking at him levelly*)
I'm calling your bluff. What is?

DR. NO (*after slightest pause, looking at him levelly*)
Ultimate Control . . . Complete . . . All-Powerful . . . of the world . . . and beyond.

And Dr. No's conspiracy is no longer to blow up the Panama Canal but to "topple" American space rockets launched from Cape Canaveral with a powerful radio beam powered by a nuclear reactor. This was closer to the book, where he has been interfering with American test missiles launched from a nearby base on Turks Island.

The introduction of SPECTRE had the effect of detaching the narrative from the ideological and geopolitical contexts of the Cold War. The criminal syndicate had emerged from the unmade film project *James Bond of the Secret Service* on which Fleming had worked with Kevin McClory and screenwriter Jack Whittingham: Fleming subsequently incorporated it into *Thunderball*. It seems reasonable to assume that its adoption for *Dr. No* was down to Maibaum, who had written a script of *Thunderball* before *Dr. No* was confirmed as the first film. The use of SPECTRE in preference to the Soviet Union or Red China has usually been explained as part of a strategy to depoliticize the content of the Bond films for both economic and ideological reasons. There had been a cycle of anti-Communist thrillers in Hollywood in the 1950s—including *I Was a Communist for the FBI* (1951), *Big Jim McLean* (1952), and *Blood Alley* (1955)—but none had scored at the box office. Nor had their British equivalents such as *High Treason* (1951) and *The Man Between* (1953). According to Broccoli: "We decided to steer 007 and the scripts clear of politics. Bond would have no identifiable political affiliation. None of the protagonists would be the stereotyped Iron Curtain or 'inscrutable Oriental' villain."[22] This direction was also supported by United Artists. David Picker cabled the producers early during preparation of the first sequel to *Dr. No*: "DISCUSSED VILLAIN FROM RUSSIA WITH LOVE AND UNANIMOUS FEELING IS SHOULD BE SPECTRE OR SIMILAR THIRD FORCE AND NOT RUSSIANS AS IN BOOK."[23]

The introduction of Felix Leiter into *Dr. No* was also more than just a cosmetic change. Leiter—Bond's trusted friend and colleague from the CIA—appears in six of the books: *Casino Royale, Live and Let Die, Diamonds Are Forever, Goldfinger, Thunderball*, and the as-yet-unwritten *The Man with the Golden Gun*. Leiter's presence in *Dr. No* was not because Bond needed an ally: that role was taken by Quarrel. Kingsley Amis offers a perceptive analysis of Leiter's role in the books in *The James Bond Dossier*:

> The point of Felix Leiter, such a nonentity as a piece of characterization, is that he, the American, takes orders from Bond, the Britisher, and that Bond is constantly doing better than he, showing himself, not braver or more devoted, but smarter, wittier, tougher, more resourceful, the incarnation of little old England with her quiet ways and shoe-string budget wiping the eye of great big global-tentacled multi-billion-dollar-appropriating America.[24]

This also seems a useful way of understanding Leiter's presence in *Dr. No*. On the one hand, the film (in all its drafts) focused the conspiracy more directly toward the United States than did the book: this mandated the introduction of the CIA man into the film (figure 3.1). On the other hand, Leiter's role is subordinate to Bond's and this may be seen as a means of asserting British leadership in the Anglo-American alliance in the same way as the books. In this context, it is significant that Leiter's role gradually diminished over the various drafts from being involved in the expedition to Crab Key in the first

FIGURE 3.1 The introduction of Felix Leiter (Jack Lord) was a means of orienting the film more towards the United States. *Dr. No* (Danjaq LLC/United Artists Corporation, 1962).

full script to being absent at the climax in the fourth draft screenplay ("Leiter's a bit late with his cavalry . . . To hell with him anyway").

Another culturally significant shift was the introduction of more sexual opportunities for Bond. Amis points out that Fleming's Bond is usually a one-girl-per-book man. (This is mostly correct though there are a few exceptions.[25]) However, the various script drafts make it clear that the screen Bond would be more promiscuous than his literary counterpart. From the very first draft, Maibaum and Mankowitz devised a scene to introduce Bond at a London casino (later identified as Les Ambassadeurs), where he flirts with a woman called Sylvia. Bond is called away to Secret Service headquarters, but finds Sylvia in his apartment when he returns home prior to leaving for

Jamaica, offering to repay her "debt of honor." The early treatments also had Bond consummating his relationship with Honey before the end of the film: "They bathe in the waterfall to wash off the mud of their swampy trek. Presumably naked, we leave them waiting for the dark with several hours in which to explore whatever erotic possibilities can be discovered behind waterfalls." In the fourth draft screenplay, Bond and Honey do not lie down together until the very end, but Miss Taro provides another sexual encounter in the middle section of the film. In this sense *Dr. No*—perhaps by accident—developed the "girl formula" that future screenwriter Roald Dahl recounted was explained to him by the producers when preparing *You Only Live Twice* (1967):

> So you put in three girls. No more and no less. Girl number one is pro-Bond. She stays around roughly through the first reel of the picture. Then she is bumped off by the enemy, preferably in Bond's arms . . . Girl number two is anti-Bond. She works for the enemy and stays around throughout the middle third of the picture. She must capture Bond, and Bond must save himself by bowling her over with sheer sexual magnetism . . . Girl number three is violently pro-Bond. She occupies the final third of the picture and she must on no account be killed. Nor must she permit Bond to take any lecherous liberties with her until the very end of the story. We keep that for the fade-out.[26]

In this analogy, Sylvia is "girl number one" (though she is saved the indignity of being "bumped off by the enemy" and returns in *From Russia With Love*). Miss Taro is "girl number two" in the enemy's service, and Honey is "girl number three."

The greater sexual opportunity afforded for Bond in the films was quite evidently a conscious decision. It needs to be understood in relation to the relaxation of film censorship and to changing attitudes toward sex in society at large. Both the British Board of Film Censors and the US Production Code Administration were becoming more liberal in terms of what they would allow by the early 1960s: full nudity was still banned (except for the exploitation genre of documentary-style "nudist" films), but the censors had more or less given up on trying to enforce the principle that sex should be presented within a moral framework. Bond's casual use of women in the films is in contrast to the books, where he is more often characterized as being protective and even chivalrous in his treatment of them. This is particularly evident in his relationship with Honeychile in *Dr. No*. More generally the early Bond pictures—and other British films of the 1960s such as *Tom Jones* (1963), *Darling* (1965), and *Alfie* (1966)—were markers of the emergence of the "permissive society": a new openness and frankness in sexual relations that cast aside the prurient Victorianism that (depending upon one's point of view) had acted either as a shackle or a safeguard for the previous century. Philip Larkin's oft-quoted line from "Annus Mirabilis" ("Sexual intercourse began in nineteen sixty-three . . . Between the end of the Chatterley ban/And the Beatles' first LP") eloquently expresses the social Zeitgeist. The early Bond films belong to the same historical moment.

The final preproduction script of *Dr. No* was a "Fifth Draft Screenplay" dated January 8, 1962.[27] This is the first script to have a different writing credit: the names on the document are Maibaum, Mankowitz, and J. M. Harwood. In all probability the credit suggests that this was a Maibaum-Mankowitz script revised by Harwood. The Irish-born Johanna Harwood—variously described as a "girl playwright" (Maibaum) and a "continuity girl" (Young)—was a graduate of the prestigious Paris film school IDHEC (Institut des hautes études cinématographiques) and had worked as a continuity supervisor in Britain and the Republic of Ireland during the 1950s. Her credits included *The Red Beret* (which is presumably what Young was referring to when he described her as "my continuity girl on a previous picture") and Orson Welles's *Mr. Arkadin* (1955). Harwood was evidently well acquainted with Fleming's work: she had written a short Bond pastiche for the magazine *Nursery World* imagining Bond as a precocious child who competes with his nanny in a high-stakes game of Snap.[28]

Melanie Williams contends that Harwood's contribution to the scripting of *Dr. No* "may well have been disregarded or downplayed for reasons connected with her gender."[29] This is entirely plausible. At the same time, however, it is curious that Harwood's name is included on the Fifth Draft Screenplay but not Berkely Mather's. Mather must have contributed to this draft, as the United Artists records include a request for an advance cash payment of £500 for him dated December 12, 1961. (Harwood is not included.[30]) Mather was the pen name of J. E. W. Davies, author of *The Achilles Affair*, *The Pass Beyond Kashmir*, and other spy thrillers. Ian Fleming had provided an endorsement for the latter book: "One of the adventure story writers whose work I shall in future buy 'sight unseen.'"[31]

Harwood averred that Mather was brought in to "masculinize" the dialogue.³²

The main difference between the Fifth Draft Screenplay and previous versions is that it introduces some (though not all) of Bond's offhand one-liners, such as the scene where he drives up to Government House with a dead heavy in the back seat of his car and tells the duty sentry, "Make sure he doesn't get away." This would suggest that Harwood (or Harwood and Mather) were responsible for the injection of intentional humor into the script. It provides a corrective to Young's claim that "[an] awful lot of the funny things in *Dr. No* were knocked up on the set. I suppose I did half, and he [Sean Connery] did at least half himself. He had some very sweet lines and ideas: some of them worked and some of them didn't."³³

However, the Fifth Draft Screenplay reveals that the producers were still unsure about one key scene not from the book: the moment where Bond kills Professor Dent. This uncertainty is evident in the fact that the script includes—somewhat unusually—three different versions of the same scene. In Scene 135, Bond, following the arrest of Miss Taro, is waiting in the dark, knowing that an assassin is on the way to kill him. He has arranged pillows in the bed to resemble a sleeping body. Dent arrives and shoots what he believes is the sleeping Bond; the script describes "silenced 'coughing' shots which done properly can sound horrible." Bond then holds Dent at gunpoint and interrogates him, while Dent, having dropped his gun on the rug, attempts to retrieve it, apparently unnoticed by Bond. The scene is described thus:

BOND
Who are you working for, Professor?

DENT
(*we get the impression he is talking to distract BOND's attention as he moves towards his gun*)
I may as well tell you . . . you won't live to use the information . . . I'm working for . . .

He makes a sudden swift movement towards his gun, picks it up and levels it at BOND. As his finger tightens on the trigger.

DENT (contd.) (*triumphantly*)
. . . Dr. No!

His finger tightens on the trigger, but the hammer clicks down on an empty chamber.

BOND
Only six bullets in a Smith and Wesson, Professor . . . and I counted them . . .

He raises his own gun deliberately, squeezes the trigger. DENT spins backwards as if somebody has kicked him, slamming up against a flimsy Chinese table and crushing it as he collapses. He rolls right over onto his back . . . brings his legs up under his chin in an agonised convulsion . . . shoots them straight out . . . and then lies still. BOND raises and crosses to him. He doesn't need

> to examine him closely, knowing exactly where he's hit him. He blows the fumes away from his gun, and goes to the bed, where we see two interlaced "forms" made from the bolster and pillow. They are ripped by shots, charred round the edges of the holes, and feathers are scattered. BOND picks up the phone and dials. His eyes are hard.

The scene as described presents Bond as a cold-blooded killer: he shoots Dent in the knowledge that the other man's gun is empty. This was a departure for the film: Fleming's Bond had never killed in quite such a ruthless fashion. Probably mindful that this might prove problematic from a censorship point of view, the screenplay included two alternative versions of the scene. In the first, Dent's gun is not empty: he fires at Bond but misses, while Bond fires and hits Dent. In the second, Dent goes for his gun but is shot by Bond before he reaches it. Both the alternatives could be understood as Bond acting in self-defense. It is not clear whether the alternative versions were filmed. In the finished film, Bond does shoot Dent in cold blood ("That's a Smith and Wesson—and you've had your six") but goes even further than the script by shooting him again in the back (figure 3.2). The additional shot is unnecessary and therefore gratuitous. There is evidence that Bond originally continued to fire: the British Board of Film Censors insisted that the scene be trimmed to only one nonfatal shot.[34]

It is generally agreed that Harwood contributed one of the film's most memorable moments, a visual joke that is not in the script. This is the moment when Bond performs a double-take when he recognizes Francisco de Goya's portrait of the Duke

FIGURE 3.2 A new scene written for the film presented Bond as assassin: "That's a Smith & Wesson—and you've had your six." *Dr. No* (Danjaq LLC/United Artists Corporation, 1962).

of Wellington in Dr. No's apartments. This painting had been stolen from the National Gallery in London in August 1961.[35] Following the release of *Dr. No*, the society columnist "Atticus" of the *Sunday Times* reported that this moment "brought a round of applause at the Press show" and suggested that the painting's inclusion—the producers paid £50 to the National Gallery for the right to reproduce a copy—was Harry Saltzman's idea. (The item may have been planted by Ian Fleming, who had once been the man behind "Atticus" and maintained a close connection with the newspaper even after stepping down from its editorial team in 1961.) This prompted a rejoinder from Harwood: "It was I who invented the Goya joke in the film *Dr. No*. I am glad Atticus appreciated it."[36] Another correspondent pointed out that a similar joke about the stolen Goya had already been used on *Candid Camera* and in several newspaper cartoons.

One scene not in any version of the script was filmed but ended up not being included in the film. The fourth and fifth drafts have Bond rescuing Honey from the same hotel/prison where they had been imprisoned earlier: "HONEY is standing in a pathetic last stance . . . a bottle of whisky upraised as a weapon. She looks unbelievably at them [two attackers] . . . then half collapses. BOND dashes forwards and catches her. Being BOND, he also manages to catch the bottle before it hits the floor." At some point during the studio shooting, it was decided to attempt to film Honey being staked out for the crabs as per the novel. The daily progress reports confirm that the scene in the "Crab Room" was shot on Friday, March 30 and Monday, April 2. There is some anecdotal evidence that this scene was included in the film at the time of its trade show for critics: it was mentioned in reviews by Alexander Walker (*Evening Standard*) and Leonard Mosley (*Daily Express*). The latter wrote: "The beautiful blonde has been shackled to the ground and a couple of Oriental villains are grinning lasciviously as poison spiders [*sic*] crawl over her limbs."[37] The scene was reportedly cut from the film because it looked risible on the screen (and not—as a later review in *The Spectator* suggested—at the insistence of the censors).[38] Instead, it appears, without any explanation, that Honey has simply been left to drown, as she is shackled to the floor in front of some sort of sluice gate (figure 3.3).

Penelope Houston, writing following Fleming's death, averred that the best qualities of his writing were inherently unfilmable:

If the books are compellingly readable, it's for all sorts of non-adaptable reasons. Ian Fleming was not, like Graham Greene in the mood of his "entertainments," a master of the almost self-consciously cinematic image. The things he did best were things that the cinema does badly ... He was very good on the sensations of fast driving: the cinema can't cope with this, perhaps because of the problem of where just to fit the camera, so that you are liable to end up with no more than screaming tyres on the sound track, close-ups of hands on the wheel, and windscreen views of the road. You can do all sorts of things with cars in the cinema, except communicate the sensation of actually driving one.[39]

This is true—but only to an extent. Fleming's writing does indeed excel in the description of sensory experiences: in this

FIGURE 3.3 Honey (Ursula Andress) staked out for the crabs. *Dr. No* (Danjaq LLC/United Artists Corporation, 1962).

context his books recall the fiction of John Buchan, with their frequent references to physical sensations (exhaustion, hunger, pain) as well as their sense of pace and movement. But on a structural level, the novel of *Dr. No* was very much the template for the finished film, and many scenes remained more or less intact.

The scripting history of *Dr. No* demonstrates the film industry adage that scripts are not written but rewritten: no single writer had agency (unlike the novel) and the final screenplay was the outcome of multiple inputs. It also provides an exemplary case study of how the source material was revised and adapted in line with the industrial and ideological determinants of the film industry. This saw much of the sadism that critics had detected in the novel removed or at least substantially toned down (the philosophical discussions about pain and endurance are omitted, and Bond's escape through the ventilation shaft is a much less harrowing experience than in the novel), though the sex and snobbery remained. It also saw the plot removed from the Cold War background of the book and realigned geopolitically. Furthermore, the adaptation process for *Dr. No* was unusual insofar as the successive drafts brought the script progressively closer to the source text. This would tend to support Richard Maibaum's suggestion that the success of the early Bond films was rooted in Fleming's originals. And this, in turn, provides further evidence that the ultimate success of *Dr. No* was no happy accident, but rather was the outcome of a shrewd assessment of the commercial potential of the books.

Chapter Four

UNDERNEATH THE MANGO TREE

DR. NO WENT before the cameras in Jamaica on the morning of Tuesday, January 16, 1962. The first scene to be shot was Bond's arrival at Kingston airport (figure 4.1). It was an overcast day and the unit had to return the following morning to complete the setups.[1] *Dr. No* was therefore behind schedule on location from the very start. It never caught up. The first week saw the unit shooting the scenes in which Bond is tailed from the airport and overpowers the imposter chauffeur "Mr. Jones" and exteriors at Morgan's Harbor, where Bond meets Quarrel. A report in the *Daily Gleaner*—the Kingston newspaper that Bond reads in the novel—was distinctly unimpressed with what it had observed of the early shooting:

> If the first day's shooting was any indication of the quality of the finished product, *Dr. No* promises to be a slapdash and rather regrettable picture . . . I can foresee quite a bit of

trouble for the producers of *Dr. No*. And I will stick my neck out by predicting that the critics will have a field-day with the title of the film. What I have heard of the dialogue is appalling.[2]

As one of the first major feature films to include extensive location shooting in Jamaica—hitherto Walt Disney's *20,000 Leagues Under the Sea* (1954) was probably the biggest film to have been shot on the island—*Dr. No* attracted a good deal of coverage in the local press. It was evidently a source of local pride that the film recruited a significant number of Jamaican actors: these included Reggie Carter as "Mr. Jones," Marguerite LeWars (the current "Miss Jamaica") as Annabel Chung, the photographer who appears at the airport and again

FIGURE 4.1 Principal photography of *Dr. No* commenced at Kingston Airport on January 16, 1962. *Dr. No* (Danjaq LLC/United Artists Corporation, 1962).

at Pus-Feller's nightclub, and Louis Blaazer as the Principal Secretary Pleydell-Smith. Several of those cast were not professional actors: Timothy Moxon, uncredited in the film as Strangways, was a commercial pilot; Lester Prendergast, who played Pus-Feller, was an actual nightclub owner; and William Foster-Davis, cast as Superintendent Duff, was a local businessman. Dolores Keator reportedly got the part of Mary Trueblood because she owned the house where the scene of Mary's murder was shot.³ The recruitment of local talent was no doubt partly an economic decision, as wages would be lower (extras were paid £5 a day) and there would be cost savings on transport and accommodation. But it should also be seen to some degree as a strategy to ensure cultural authenticity for the Jamaican scenes. The *Daily Gleaner* reported that Monty Norman, "who is to write the music for the film, will use local bands as far as possible" and that Terence Young "will be interviewing local artists at the Copacabana club."⁴ Byron Lee and the Dragonaires, a well-known local calypso and ska band, appeared as the house musicians at Pus-Feller's, as did reggae musician Count Prince Miller, who performs his signature dance routine to "Jump Up, Jamaica" in the same sequence.

Dr. No was recognized as a major opportunity to showcase Jamaica as a location for runaway filmmaking. Hollywood had embraced overseas production enthusiastically in the 1950s and the trend continued into the 1960s. It was not just local color and scenery that attracted filmmakers, but also the cheaper production costs and the availability of local subsidies or tax incentives. (Jamaica had introduced such a scheme for filmmaking as early as 1948.) By the middle of February, the *Daily*

Gleaner had overcome its initial skepticism and was reporting positively about the film unit's contribution to the local economy: "The filming of Ian Fleming's book *Dr. No* in Jamaica has brought many pounds into the island. A considerable number of Jamaicans have been employed—as supporting actors and actresses, as technicians and as labourers. In addition to this, the publicity for Jamaica will be splendid." The reporter was particularly taken with the film's co-star—who arrived on location on Monday, January 29—and set the tone for much of the publicity material around *Dr. No* by commenting that "many of us have seen the leading lady, Miss Ursula Andress, in a bikini: a sight as sensational and perhaps even more stimulating than such natural splendours as Niagara Falls and [the] Grand Canyon."[5] Andress's famous entrance wearing the said bikini was shot at Laughing Waters beach on Jamaica's northern coast on Thursday, February 8 (figure 4.2).

The historical context added a particular significance to the production. The film was shot during Jamaica's last days of British rule: this colony since 1655 would become independent on August 6, 1962. To that extent, the film's colonial trappings, including scenes shot at Government House and at the Queen's Club, would be anachronistic by the time of its release. Jamaica's transition to independence had been signaled in September 1961, when a referendum held by the government of Prime Minister Norman Manley resulted in Jamaica's withdrawal from the Federation of the West Indies. A general election in April 1962—in which the presence of suspected "Russian spy ships" in Kingston Harbor fed into concerns about security—saw Sir Alexander Bustamante's Jamaica Labour Party defeat

FIGURE 4.2 The meeting between Bond and Honey was shot at Laughing Waters, Jamaica, on February 8, 1962. *Dr. No* (Danjaq LLC/United Artists Corporation, 1962).

Manley's People's National Party. The UK Parliament passed the Jamaica Independence Act on July 19 and Jamaica became an independent state on August 6 while maintaining membership in the British Commonwealth. James Robertson has analyzed *Dr. No* in its Jamaican contexts: he argues that "it caught current transitions as Jamaicans sought to comprehend the shift from life in a minor British colony to citizenship in an independent state that would need to fit into the unequal power relations of the cold war while producing commodities for multinational companies and developing a mass tourism product."[6]

John Pearson's biography of Ian Fleming avers that the author "refused to become too involved with either the film or the filmmakers."[7] However, Fleming was more closely involved in the filming of *Dr. No* than the official biography would suggest. He personally recommended Chris Blackwell—son of his Jamaican neighbor and confidante Blanche Blackwell—as a location manager and local "fixer."[8] A contemporary report in the *Sunday Times* (possibly planted by Fleming) intimated that "Fleming has managed rather splendidly to borrow a luxury Jamaican estate that Henry Ford once wanted to buy as a location for the film. He flies out next month to keep an eye on things generally."[9] The "luxury estate" was probably the mansion owned by Lord Brownlow that doubled as the interior of Government House when the unit was denied permission to film in the real location.[10] United Artists' records indicate that the studio had envisaged a larger role for Fleming in the making and promotion of *Dr. No*. UA's publicity department suggested producing a promotional featurette for television that could "show Fleming and Connery demonstrating the various aspects of Bondsmanship, including handling a Biretta [sic], handling a woman, mixing martinis, ordering a gourmet dinner etc." It also suggested arranging a stopover for Fleming in Washington "to visit with the Kennedys" and an appearance on the popular late-night program *The Jack Paar Show* on his return via New York "because he would have his experience making the motion picture to relate." However, neither of these ideas were realized. Nor was the most intriguing suggestion: that Fleming should have a part in the film and that he would be "particularly apt as M, the head of the intelligence service."[11]

Fleming was a frequent visitor on location and seems to have been smitten with Ursula Andress, for whom he wrote a "cameo" in *On Her Majesty's Secret Service*, which he was writing while *Dr. No* was being shot (figure 4.3).[12] A letter from the author's

FIGURE 4.3 Ian Fleming was a frequent visitor on location in Jamaica. Courtesy of the Everett Collection/Alamy.

wife, Ann Fleming, to Evelyn Waugh provides eyewitness testimony of an unexpected interruption to the filming:

> On location with the film company producing *Dr. No*, they were shooting a beach scene, the hero and heroine cowering behind a ridge of sand to escape death from a machine gun mounted on a deep-sea fishing craft borrowed from a neighbouring hotel and manned by communist negroes [*sic*]. The sand ridge was planted with French letters full of explosives—by magic mechanism they blew up the sand in little puffs. The machine gun gave mild pops but I was assured this would be improved on the sound track; all this

endeavour was wasted because unluckily a detachment of [the] American Navy entered the bay in speed launches and buggered it all up . . . [They] told us they were on French leave from Cuba and were in search of drink and women.¹³

This account in fact conflates two successive days: the daily progress reports indicate the interruption due to "other boats getting in shot" as occurring the day after the special-effects shots of the machine-gun bullets.¹⁴ Other accounts of the same incident have it that it was the Fleming party—including author Peter Quennell and poet Stephen Spender as well as the Flemings themselves—who accidentally interrupted the filming when they wandered into the background of the shot.¹⁵

The completion guarantor Film Finances was monitoring the production from London via progress and cost reports and letters from Harry Saltzman. (All the correspondence in the Film Finances Archive is from Saltzman: Broccoli is an invisible presence.) Its first intervention was to remind Eon Productions on February 12 that the fee for the guarantee was overdue.¹⁶ It was soon apparent that the film was slipping behind schedule: attempting to make up the time, the unit worked two Sundays (involving expensive overtime payments) on February 4 and 18 . On the latter day, Saltzman wrote to Robert Garrett:

> We have encountered many problems on this location. Basically, the biggest problem is the "manana" attitude of the local people and the fact that they do not keep their promises to their contracts and this has caused quite costly delays.

For example, on one day, out of five boats required, four of the motors broke down. The deals with the boatmen were for boats in working order and their stock answer was: "The boat worked perfectly yesterday." . . . To put it mildly we have been gulled and taken in due to the complacency and complete and utter inefficiency of the locals. This has not been merely directed to us, but we see this evidenced by all the business people and firms working in Jamaica.[17]

It was no doubt a good thing that Saltzman's opinion of the Jamaican labor force was not picked up by the local press or chamber of commerce: this was not the impression they would have wanted in their efforts to encourage other film producers to come to the island. Against this, however, should be set Saltzman's reputation for leaving bills to contractors unpaid. This had emerged in relation to his film *The Iron Petticoat* in 1956 and was still evidently an issue with *Dr. No*: a local solicitor was left chasing Eon Productions for payment of £432 13s. in respect to damage to a motor boat "apparently abandoned by your employees and subsequently rescued by two fishermen."[18]

The intent behind Saltzman's letter was to reassure Garrett that the film was going well despite the difficulties and to allay Film Finances' anxieties about Terence Young. He told him: "I must say Terence has behaved tremendously well, despite all our misgivings and I honestly must say that none of the hold-ups have been due to his proclivity from [sic] procrastination." Garrett, however, was not taken in. He annotated with four exclamation marks a paragraph where Saltzman said:

The only thing about Terence that hasn't changed is his "grand seigneur" way of living. He has spent money personally like water and has charmed us out of over £500 in cash advances and we still don't know what his various bills around the Island will come to. However, we are recovering his advances by deductions from his salary cheques sent to MCA.

Saltzman acknowledged that the contingency allowance in the budget had already been raided, but assured Garrett that the film was otherwise in good shape: "In spite of all the ulcer-making frustrating situations and the invasion of a good deal of our contingency fund, the stuff we have shot here is tremendously impressive and I think well worth our troubles . . . Both Cubby and myself feel very optimistic about the commercial possibilities of this picture."

To be entirely fair, many of the problems encountered on location for *Dr. No* were not down to Terence Young. The causes of delays are documented in the daily progress reports. There was the usual range of minor accidents and illnesses: Ursula Andress fell and grazed her knee on the first morning at Laughing Waters, Anthony Dawson contracted gastroenteritis, director of photography Ted Moore was treated for an "infected foot," electrician William Duke "fell in river and hurt hand," and assistant director Clive Reed was bitten by one of the police dogs used for the film and had to be taken to a hospital for inoculation. John Kitzmiller was the worst affected: he experienced swelling to his hand while filming the scene at Morgan's Harbour during the first week, as is evident in the awkward way in which Quarrel holds his right hand in those scenes. He received physiotherapy for the rest of the shoot. He also hurt his foot on a rock while shooting the scene at Dunn River Falls on the penultimate day on location. Other delays were caused by mechanical faults to the "dragon" vehicle and the Royal Navy motor launch that appeared in the final scene. A half-day's filming outside Government House (January 26) was "held up . . . by presence of Governor who had not left as expected." However, the most common reason for losing time was inclement weather: the progress reports for January 19, January 30, January 31, February 7, February 8, February 16, and February 18 all include "bad light" or "waiting for sun" or a similar variant as the cause of delay, while "rough seas" affected two days filming at sea (February 2 and 3). When the unit left for London on a BOAC charter flight on Friday, February 23, *Dr. No* was six days over schedule and was running an estimated £20,000 over budget.[19]

Nevertheless, Young was concerned that he was going to be blamed for the delays on location. He defended his record in a letter written shortly after completion of the film in which he was at pains to rebut the charge of being a slow and spendthrift director:

> To cut it short I would only say (and I know how unBritish and ungentlemanly it is to blow a trumpet) the hard facts are that if I had not been making the picture, it would have gone over by more than ten days—much, much more. I happen to have made more location pictures than any two other British directors—has anyone ever noticed the incidence with which location films get into trouble—and if I had not known how

to improvise, how to change one's whole method of shooting in an emergency, how not to get into trouble by shooting more than two master angles, and knowing how I could cover up by finishing a sequence later in the studio, then we could have got quite seriously into trouble on this film. And it would not have been the producers' fault either, because they did do what was possible, but they could not arrange the weather, or change the Jamaican temperament.[20]

The context for this letter (to his solicitor) was Young's complaint about what he considered his "shabby" treatment by Film Finances over holding part of his salary in escrow (even though Young himself had agreed to this prior to shooting). His rhetorical question about the incidence of location films getting into trouble had indeed been noted by Film Finances—especially when they were directed by Terence Young! *The Red Beret*, *Safari*, and *Action of the Tiger* had all run over schedule on location. Garrett pointed out in response that Young had approved a schedule that made insufficient allowance for the likelihood of weather disruption and pointed out that prior to leaving for location "he attended a meeting with us here at which we were as usual at pains to point out the hazards of locations and the fact that we just do not believe this story that you can rely upon good weather anywhere."[21]

In the meantime, further problems were emerging around the studio shooting. The most worrying of these had been signaled by production designer Ken Adam while the unit was still on location in Jamaica. In December, Adam had provided a letter required for the completion guarantee to the effect that the budget allocations for set construction and props were "adequate for the work indicated in script and budget."[22] The budget allowed £12,500 for set construction (£8,000 for labor and £4,500 for materials) and another £4,500 for props and set dressing. However, on February 1, 1962, Adam wrote to Saltzman to inform him that "due to various circumstances, the cost of studio sets will in my opinion be approximately £17,000. Cost of props for studio set dressing will be approximately between £6,000 and £7,000. This is merely a note to make quite certain that you have realised this."[23] Adam's DVD commentary for *Dr. No* claimed that he was given the okay by the producers for the additional expenditure on sets, which would be met from the contingency.[24] This was not known to Film Finances at the time: it is very likely that the guarantor was deliberately left in the dark. Garrett would certainly have objected to such "improvements" to the film: the practice of spending more to enhance the production values when such expenditure had not been included in the budget and specification on which the guarantee had been agreed was frowned upon most severely.[25]

Following the locations in Jamaica, *Dr. No* went on the studio floor at Pinewood on Monday, February 26. This time it was the British weather that caused a delay: there was a late start to filming "due to snow and ice on roads."[26] The first scene was Bond's briefing by M. Bernard Lee (M) and Peter Burton (Major Boothroyd) completed their scenes in two days, Lois Maxwell (Miss Moneypenny) in one. The studio shooting continued until April 3. The schedule had to be extended to include certain interiors that it had not been possible to complete on location. Young had been at pains to defend his ability to improvise on location, but he now fell behind in the studio, too. Film Finances noted "that in the studio he went seven days over schedule plus two days' further work. It might also be pertinent to ask to what extent Terence's ideas or demands contributed to the vast over-costs on the sets."[27] A production diary compiled by Eon claimed that the studio shooting period had averaged two minutes and twenty-two seconds of screen time per day and suggested that it was "questionable if any other major film, with a similar budget, has ever accomplished the feat of shooting on 22 major different sets in 23 days. This is practically television or 'B' picture scheduling, and on this film it was necessary, and had to be done."[28]

The studio shooting again highlights how anecdotal accounts and archival records of filmmaking are often at variance. Young—having already shot "the greatest woman's entrance in a picture"—also shot what he considered the second-best man's entrance (after Omar Sharif's in *Lawrence of Arabia*): Connery's "Bond . . . James Bond" moment (figure 4.4). He said that he modelled the scene, where the back of Bond's head and his hands are seen before he speaks his first line, on Paul Muni's star buildup in *Juarez* (1938).[29] Eunice Gayson, cast in the role of Bond's paramour Sylvia Trench, recalled that a nervous Connery repeatedly fluffed his big line:

> My first scene with Sean was inside the casino at the baccarat table and to say he was nervous would be an understatement . . . Nine takes later Sean had gone through every permutation of "Bond, James Bond" you could think of, from "Bond, Sean Bond" to "Sean, Bond James" to "James, I mean

Bond James" and so on . . . Terence was silently pulling his hair out in frustration. It was now approaching lunchtime and it seemed like a good idea to take a break. Terence took me to one side and said, "Eunice, please take Sean down to the restaurant and give him a couple of drinks. Calm him down and then we'll go again."[30]

According to Gayson's account, Connery returned to the set three vodkas later and "nailed it in one." The daily production report for that day, however, offers a rather more prosaic account of the day's filming: "Serious delays today due to emulsion pickup in gate."[31]

It was during the studio period that the full extent of the overspending became apparent. The weekly cost statements

FIGURE 4.4 Sean Connery's "Bond . . . James Bond" introduction was shot on Stage D at Pinewood Studios on March 2, 1962. *Dr. No* (Danjaq LLC/United Artists Corporation, 1962).

indicated that the film was over budget in several areas—publicity, music, studio rentals, and insurances—but the one that most concerned Film Finances was set construction, which by the statement of March 9 was around £14,000 above the original estimate. On March 15, Film Finances' joint managing director, Bernard Smith, "had a meeting with the producers to ascertain the true position." He reported that "Unfortunately, the situation is worse than I had anticipated and the film will now exceed its schedule by eleven days and the cost position is estimated to be £22,700 over budget."[32] The following day, Garrett wrote to Saltzman, telling him that Film Finances were now "very disturbed" about the film's progress:

> Our first and most serious criticism is that you should have decided (without consultation with us) to embark on an obviously more ambitious set building programme at a time when it was clear that certain setbacks on the location had already gone a long way towards exhausting your contingency. Not only has this involved a very considerable increase in construction costs but it has entailed additional increases in other spheres such as power, lighting, etc. It seems to us also, unless the strictest control is maintained, likely that the increased size and scope of the sets may well lead to further loss of time in the studio shooting . . . I must ask you and Cubby to take all possible measures of economy and above all, to see that the schedule position does not deteriorate further.[33]

Saltzman replied, somewhat disingenuously, that there had been no change to the set-building program, which he claimed had been agreed to before the unit left for Jamaica, and averred that the overspending on sets was due to the cost of labor, which he blamed on Pinewood Studios:

> Actually, if you look at the Cost Sheets closely, where we went tremendously over was in production labour which will amount to well over 100% of budget, whereas in construction materials our excess over budget is about 30%. I am going over the overtime labour bills and I find these enormous . . . It has been both Cubby's and my experience that this always happens when a studio has only one film on the go.[34]

Dr. No completed principal photography on April 3. The studio sequences were seven days over schedule and the film as a whole was twelve days over and estimated to be £46,434 over budget.[35] It was at this point that Film Finances decided to exercise its right to take over the production to ensure its timely and economical completion. This was a clause of the completion guarantee that provided security for the guarantor against films running out of control: it was regarded very much as a last resort and had rarely been invoked in the course of the 327 films guaranteed by Film Finances prior to *Dr. No*.[36] The fact that this picture had completed principal photography made no difference: Film Finances' experience was that overcosts had a tendency to increase during post-production. On April 3, Garrett—as was his custom, including with the formal notice of takeover a personal letter that was almost apologetic in tone—told Saltzman: "As an old friend I am sorry we have found it necessary to take over the production of *Dr. No*. Quite frankly,

I feel this is the only way in which we can make sure that the concluding stages of the picture are carried out with the maximum economy and that the overcost is not further increased."[37] What it meant in practice was that Film Finances' approval was required for any further expenditure and the company's representative became cosignatory on all checks drawn on the production account. When Garrett heard that the producers had not given notice to some crew members, a consequence of which was to incur an extra week of salary costs, he commented privately that it "seems quite typical of their attitude and makes one feel that we should certainly not be in any hurry to remove our direct control."[38]

Eon now provided, at Film Finances' request, a schedule and cost estimate for necessary shots that remained uncompleted. The producers estimated that two days of additional shooting would be required, at a cost of £2,069.[39] This was reduced to one day of pickups and inserts that were shot at Pinewood on Thursday, April 26. These included the back-projection shots of Bond at the wheel of his Sunbeam Alpine for the car chase (figure 4.5), Bond knocking out one of Dr. No's guards, and the close-ups of the tarantula crawling over Bond's shoulder (for which Connery's stunt double Bob Simmons was paid £25). The distinguished cameraman Otto Heller—whose films included *Queen of Spades*, *Richard III*, and *Peeping Tom* and who would later shoot *The Ipcress File* for Saltzman—stepped in for the day when Ted Moore was unavailable. "Rosie" the tarantula was paid £14 10s. for her small but vital role.[40]

With the shooting complete, it was time for a post-mortem into the reasons for *Dr. No*'s running so far over budget. The

FIGURE 4.5 Sean Connery's close-ups for the car chase were shot on a day of "pick ups" on April 26, 1962. *Dr. No* (Danjaq LLC/United Artists Corporation, 1962).

terms of the completion guarantee were that Film Finances would cover all reasonable overcosts due to unforeseen circumstances but that they were not responsible for "improvements" to the film that were not included in the agreed budget and where the producer had deliberately spent more. The inevitable recriminations ensued. Ken Adam's letter to Saltzman about the cost of sets came to light; this confirmed Garrett's view that Saltzman had knowingly allowed Adam to exceed the budget for set construction. Garrett put Saltzman on notice that Film Finances would take a hard line on this matter:

> We are taking a very serious view about the sets on this picture. From Ken Adam's letter it is evident that for some time prior to the 1st February, i.e. at the very outset of the

picture he had warned you that the sets and props were going to exceed the budget by approximately £7,000. A few weeks before on December 22nd Ken Adam, with whose work we are familiar and in whose judgement we trust, had written to us that he considered the budget allowance adequate. It seems therefore that it was decided at this early date to embark on a more ambitious set building operation and, although your Art Director warned you of the increase that would inevitably absorb a third of your contingency, you did not attempt to cut back on these sets.

At the various meetings, the suggestion has often been made that the increase on these sets came as a surprise and that you were entirely committed to them before you realised the effect they were going to have on the cost of the picture. We feel we cannot accept this in view of Ken Adam's warning.[41]

The final cost of sets and models on *Dr. No* was £53,835, including £18,479 for labor (against a budget of £8,000), £8,986 for materials (against a budget of £4,500), and £9,811 for props (against a budget of £4,500) (figure 4.6). As well as the sets, there were also significant overcosts on studio rentals (£8,850 over budget), power (£1,515 over), costumes (£1,003 over), travel and transport (£12,744 over), holiday and sick pay (£4,187 over) and publicity expenses (£2,193 over), though hotel and living expenses were £12,925 under budget despite Young's "grand seigneur" habits on location. A projected overcost of £1,199 on "orchestra and composer"—occasioned when John Barry was brought in to rearrange Monty Norman's "James Bond Theme"—was

FIGURE 4.6 Film Finances was concerned that the producers had knowingly exceeded their budget for sets to enhance production values. *Dr. No* (Danjaq LLC/United Artists Corporation, 1962).

reduced to £399.⁴² The audited production cost of *Dr. No* was £392,022 2s. 3d.: this represented expenditure of 21.7 percent above the final agreed budget of £322,069.⁴³

Film Finances' business model was based on the expectation that around one film in five would call upon the guarantee and that average spending above budget would be in the region of 10 percent: this was the basis on which the guarantor reinsured its risks through consequential loss policies on each film. It would recoup its advances from the box-office receipts, ranking behind the bank but ahead of the producers for recovery. The overcost on *Dr. No* was therefore twice the average. This helps to contextualize why Film Finances exercised its right to take over the film. Nevertheless, the company felt its recovery position was secure. Bernard Smith wrote in a letter to insurance underwriters Tufnell, Satterthwaite & Co.: "It would seem to be a very good action picture and, as you know, it is in colour. The distribution is being handled by United Artists on a worldwide basis and is the first of the 'James Bond' stories which have a very large reading public. Taking all these factors into account, I feel that recovery can be regarded as being very good."[44]

Even so, Film Finances was not willing to accept responsibility for the full overcost of *Dr. No*. The additional expenditure on sets remained a bone of contention. Garrett told Saltzman that "we take the view that since you decided (after receiving a warning from Ken Adam, and while there was still time to readjust matters) to go ahead with the certainty that the set budget originally approved by Adam was going to be short by £7,000, that you must make yourself responsible for providing this extra finance."[45] However, the producers were unable to find the £7,000 from their own resources at this time. Saltzman had only just repaid the final installment of the £6,500 loan that Film Finances had made through Edward Dryhurst Productions to renew his option on the Bond books. The solution was a quite unprecedented agreement whereby in consideration of the guarantor's not enforcing its demand for the producers to provide £7,000 of the overcost, Danjaq assigned it 5 percent of the producers' profits for *Dr. No* as collateral for the £7,000. Film Finances' interest in the box-office receipts of the films it guaranteed usually finished once it had recovered advances made under the guarantee: it was quite exceptional for it to have a "share" of the film beyond its usual recovery rights. Danjaq retained the right to buy back the profit share once Film

Finances had recovered the £7,000 "any time prior to the expiration of a period of 120 days commencing on the date of the first public exhibition of the Film in any part of the world."[46]

The total advances made by Film Finances for the completion of *Dr. No* amounted to £59,890.[47] This included the £7,000 for which the separate profit share agreement had been made and another £8,680 of Terence Young's fee still held in escrow. It was agreed that the outstanding amount due to Young could be claimed from United Artists as an advance against the profits; this explains why Young is included on the distributor's statements for a share of the receipts even though he did not have a percentage agreement.[48] United Artists advanced an additional £10,063 when a cost statement after the trade show of *Dr. No* indicated another cost increase.[49] Garrett explained that Film Finances was not prepared to pick up this additional cost: "The producers we understand ended up by going to United Artists and getting them to make the advance and no doubt, indirectly, indicated that they thought we were failing under our obligations . . . [In] our view the producers had been guilty in the finishing processes of the same lack of control which led to the overcost in the shooting period."[50]

The profit share agreement between Danjaq and Film Finances reflected the reality of the position in April 1962, when the eventual success of *Dr. No* was still far from assured. It was a temporary expedient at a time when the producers were short of cash and needed Film Finances' advances in order to complete the film. In any event, Film Finances did not benefit financially from their profit share. Following the release of *Dr. No* in Britain on October 5, Danjaq exercised its right to buy back the profit share. United Artists loaned Danjaq £7,000, in return for which Danjaq assigned to UA the 5 percent of its profits previously assigned to Film Finances, with eighteen months to redeem the loan.[51] Film Finances duly reassigned its share of the profits of *Dr. No* in an agreement dated February 8, 1963.[52] This still left the remaining £44,210 of Film Finances' advances toward the production to be recovered. In August 1962, Garrett had informed his colleagues that he had "told Harry Saltzman we would probably be prepared to accept a 15% discount for immediate repayment of our overage on the above film."[53] Saltzman—at that time in Kenya producing the Bob Hope–Anita Ekberg comedy *Call Me Bwana* (1963)—was not in a position to accept. However, Film Finances continued to look for a means of reducing its liabilities for *Dr. No*. In October 1962, they sold £10,000 of the recovery rights to a third party (one Muriel Carver, who seems to have been related to Film Finances' codirector Peter Hope) "in return for an immediate cash payment of £8,000."[54]

While it was not unknown for Film Finances to sell their recovery rights in films, this tended to be in cases where it was considered unlikely there would be any chance of recovering advances from the box-office receipts. This was evidently not the case with *Dr. No*, which had opened strongly in London and was reported to be doing excellent business in the provinces.[55] However, in the summer and autumn of 1962, Film Finances was facing a short-term liquidity crisis of its own. It had recently advanced £60,943 for *The Valiant* (1962), a naval war picture produced by Jon Penington's BHP Films for United Artists, and did not expect to recover its completion loan as the film had opened to mixed reviews and below-par box office.[56] And shortly after *Dr. No*, it had guaranteed two high-cost films that were now heading for potentially very large overcosts. *Lancelot and Guinevere* (1963), produced and directed by star Cornel Wilde for Universal Pictures, was a costume swashbuckler that included extensive location shooting in Yugoslavia. It exceeded its original budget (£494,746) by some 40 percent: the final cost of the film was £690,971.[57] The exceptionally high spending arose from overrunning on location—the unit had to return to complete several key sequences after the studio period—and the incompetence of the accounting department, which miscalculated the exchange rate, meaning that the unit was spending significantly more on location than they thought. Film Finances advanced over £100,000 toward its completion, but it was soon apparent that the film would not recover its costs.[58] The other problem picture was *Tom Jones* (1963). This film—produced and directed by Tony Richardson for Woodfall Films—had been budgeted at £412,374, but after ten weeks on location was already running an estimated £45,000 over budget due to "improvements" made by Richardson, who seems to have disregarded his budget the moment the cameras started turning.[59] On this occasion, the producer tried to resist Film Finances' invocation of the takeover clause. The matter was resolved through a Deed of Variation amending the original guarantee agreement whereby Woodfall indemnified Film Finances against any claim in return for payment of its no-claim bonus.[60]

Film Finances' relationship with Eon/Danjaq over *Dr. No* therefore needs to be placed in the wider context of the company's business in the early 1960s. It had provided seven guarantees for United Artists between 1960 and 1962: for *Follow That Man*, *The Girl on the Boat*, *The Valiant*, *Dr. No*, *I Could Go on Singing*, *Love Is a Ball*, and *Tom Jones*. Three of the films had called upon the guarantee—*Follow That Man*, *The Valiant*, and *Dr. No*—and until the Deed of Variation it was expected that *Tom Jones* was also heading for a large claim. Film Finances felt that "only *Dr. No* is a good recovery." Garrett summarized the problems with United Artists in an internal memorandum of January 1963:

> I understand United Artists' representative in Paris has for some time been highly critical of this company . . . If these surmises are correct, it seems to me not only is United Artists' attitude in view of past assistance we have given them extremely unfair but also, that it shows a complete lack of appreciation of the observance of those conditions which are essential if any guarantor is to continue in business and thereby be of use to distributors. Furthermore, it would indicate a lack of that co-operation which we have from other distributors and financiers in that United Artists representatives, both here and in New York, have allowed themselves to be "got round" by certain producers.[61]

The same memorandum also reveals that Film Finances had declined to guarantee *The Mouse on the Moon* (1963) on the grounds that the company thought it was underbudgeted: "It was suggested to us that even if we were right and this picture went over budget this should be a risk which we should be prepared to take for the sake of our good relations with United

Artists. We, nevertheless, did not see it in this way having recently had a number of unpleasant shocks."

A letter from Garrett to Film Finances' Italian representative, Prince Alessandro Tasca di Cutò, provides some context as to why the company did not guarantee any of the Bond pictures after *Dr. No*. It was shortly after *Dr. No* that Film Finances changed the conditions of its guarantee by requiring producers to put up part of their salaries as a security against the first overcost and, in the case of location pictures, mandating that they calculate the contingency allowance for the location period at 20 percent of the budget rather than the standard 10 percent:

> Harry Saltzman, who was counting on us giving a guarantee in respect of his film with Bob Hope, did not like these new terms and may have persuaded United Artists in New York that we were going to turn down his picture and thereby since they were already fairly heavily committed, forced them into giving their own guarantees. This is an experience which is not new to us, as it happened some years ago with two of Columbia's producers who wished to avoid the controls of a guarantee of completion.[62]

The two Columbia producers were undoubtedly Broccoli and Irving Allen: Film Finances had guaranteed eight films for Warwick Film Productions between 1953 and 1956. Most of Warwick's films had exceeded their budgets, and Allen in particular had sometimes proved a fractious and argumentative client. United Artists' records do not reveal how the completion guarantee for *From Russia with Love* was arranged, but for

Goldfinger, Saltzman and Broccoli themselves guaranteed 50 percent of any overcost above £40,000 secured against their share of the profits in all the Bond films.⁶³ The Film Finances Archive includes a letter of intent for a guarantee for *Thunderball* that, in the end, was not taken up by the producers.⁶⁴

What this demonstrates are the different priorities of the various stakeholders in *Dr. No*. On the one hand, United Artists adopted a laissez-faire approach to its producers: it would approve the budget but would otherwise defer creative decisions to those making the films. As David Picker put it: "UA would finance every film as an *independent production*. On approval of budget, script, director and cast, the producing entity would have *total creative control and final cut of the film* . . . Only if the film went over budget would UA have the right to step in and get involved creatively."⁶⁵ And—as the cases of both *Dr. No* and *Tom Jones* demonstrated—even an over-budget situation did not necessarily prompt an intervention from UA, which seems not to have been unduly troubled about the overcosts on those films. On the other hand, Film Finances had a vested interest in ensuring the economical completion of the picture: it was their responsibility to ensure that it was delivered on budget and schedule according to the agreed specification. To this extent, it did not appreciate the hands-off position that UA took as costs escalated: the guarantor felt that UA had tacitly endorsed the overcosts in the expectation that Film Finances would pick them up. This was the reason why Film Finances felt it could not extend its "no-claim bonus"—a clause whereby producers who did not make a claim on the guarantee would be entitled to a discount on their next picture—to all of UA's producers. As Garrett explained to George Ornstein,

> I do know that it has always been an arguing point with you that United Artists' producers were, so to speak, watched over by yourself and that therefore they were all to some extent part of the same production company . . . This however we never could accept, although it does not mean that we have not been very grateful to you on occasions where you have been able to bring pressure to bear on producers which has been in your interest.[66]

Of course, the commercial success of *Dr. No* meant that all parties came out of it well. Even so, there were some minor difficulties. Although the picture was reported to have recovered its production cost from its release in the United Kingdom, it took rather longer than expected for Film Finances to recover its advances. In July 1963, Garrett wrote to remind Eon Productions: "Due to the slowness of the recovery of this film, we would like to advise you that up to the end of July, the interest outstanding on our loan amounts to £2,450."[67] On October 9, 1963—a full year after the film's release in Britain—United Artists paid Film Finances £39,482 4s. 5d. in partial reimbursement of the production advances.[68] It was not until January 1964, by which time *From Russia with Love* had broken box-office records in Britain, that Film Finances was finally able to confirm that all its advances for *Dr. No* had been repaid with interest.

The last distributor's statement for *Dr. No* in the Film Finances Archive is dated February 29, 1964. This indicates a total producer's share (the amount due to the producer after the distributor has deducted fees and expenses) of US$2,138,906. This was the amount from "foreign territories," including the United Kingdom and Europe. The "domestic" market—the United States and Canada—showed further receipts of $669,182, but there was as yet no disbursement to the producers, because UA's expenses for prints, shipping, marketing, and censorship fees in North America amounted to $711,800. Even without the North American receipts, however, *Dr. No* was already showing a healthy profit. Following repayment of the production loan from the Bank of America ($949,934 including interest), reimbursement of the advances from Film Finances ($131,564) and the deduction of the agreed-upon reimbursement amount for Terence Young ($24,739), the rest of the producer's share was divided between United Artists ($442,999), Danjaq ($427,580), Ian Fleming ($22,718) and Saltzman and Broccoli personally in respect of their deferments ($20,327). There was also an additional payment of $1,500 to something called "Dorchester Establishment": this was probably for the hire of rooms at the Dorchester Hotel where Eon had its base before it leased its own offices.[69]

The success of *Dr. No*—and even more so *From Russia with Love*—strengthened the producers' hand in relation to the studio. The equal share of the profits agreed upon in the original financing and distribution contracts for the Bond pictures was revised to 60:40 in the producers' favor and an increase made in their fees for *Goldfinger*.[70] United Artists was willing to take a smaller percentage of a bigger pot: *Goldfinger*'s rental earnings amounted to nearly twice as much as those for *Dr. No* and *From Russia with Love* combined.[71] As David Picker put it: "Bond was a big franchise and UA knew an accommodation was necessary."[72] A further renegotiation of the profit share and fees took place following *Thunderball*. By 1966, the Bond pictures had earned total worldwide rentals of over $100 million. For the distributor, they were a license to print money.[73] UA was also evidently willing to guarantee completion of the films itself and had no need to call upon a third-party guarantor. However, as the production history of *Dr. No* revealed by the Film Finances Archive demonstrates, this was not the situation in 1962, when both distributor and producers had good reason to be grateful for Film Finances' role in maintaining oversight of the filmmaking process and stepping in when costs escalated. This again highlights the importance of placing *Dr. No* in its own industrial and production contexts, which were different from those of all the later Bond pictures.

Chapter Five

A BIZARRE COMEDY MELODRAMA

ONE OF THE MOST persistent myths about *Dr. No* is that it received a decidedly cool reception at a preview screening for United Artists executives in London. One of those present is reported to have remarked to the effect that "all we can lose is a million dollars" (the precise phrase and amount vary from one account to another). This anecdote seems to have originated with Harry Saltzman, who told it on numerous occasions, including for an interview with *Variety* to mark the twenty-fifth anniversary of the Bond series in 1987:

> When we had an answer print ready, there were about eight people from United Artists, including Arthur Krim, who came to see it. We started the picture at 10 a.m., and when it was over a few minutes before 12, the lights came up and nobody said anything except a man who was the head of the European operation for United Artists. He said, "The only

thing good about the picture is that we can only lose $840,000" [sic]. Then they all stood up, and Cubby and I were just shattered.[1]

An earlier version—told by Saltzman to Alexander Walker for his book *Hollywood, England*—identifies the doubtful executive as Ilya Lopert: "When we first ran the film, some genius said, 'Well, all we can lose is 950,000 dollars, Harry' . . . and Ilya Lopert gave it as his opinion that, 'It simply won't work in America, Connery will never go over.'"[2]

However, there is good reason to cast doubt on this story, which is yet another case of an oft-repeated anecdote assuming a greater degree of factual authority than it warrants. All of the archival evidence points toward United Artists' knowing from an early stage of the production that they had a highly commercial film on their hands. As early as February 1962, when *Dr. No* was still on location, George Ornstein told David Picker that "the rushes I have so far seen, are quite exciting and it begins to look as if we will have a good picture."[3] Charles Juroe, UA's vice-president in charge of publicity, concurred: "I think that *Dr. No* will be an exploitation picture with a lot of exciting elements in the picture going for it. But Saltzman acts as if it is the second coming of *Gone With the Wind* and becomes most upset if anyone considers it less than that."[4] Saltzman, for his part, told Film Finances that UA had rethought their release strategy based on what they had seen of the rushes:

We have now changed UA's thinking about the release and are shooting for an August release for this picture and it is conceivable that we might get the August Bank Holiday bookings . . . Further, United Artists intend to release this picture on a saturation-plan booking similar to *The Magnificent Seven* and they feel that from what they have seen the picture should get its entire production costs from the UK.[5]

And an internal Film Finances memorandum summarizing the difficulties over *Dr. No* pointed out that UA had advanced £10,000 toward the overcost after the trade show, which suggests the executives must have been satisfied with what they had seen:

> We had no doubt of the ultimate success of this film but we were on principle not prepared to make advances without proper justification. The producers we understand ended by going to United Artists and getting them to make the advance . . . At this point, since *Dr. No* was clearly a success, the producers' standing with United Artists was very different to what it had been in the early days.[6]

The most compelling evidence that Saltzman's account of UA's coolness toward *Dr. No* may not have been entirely true is that the reviews following the film's London trade show (at the Odeon, Haymarket) on August 31, 1962 were unanimously positive. It would be unusual for experienced studio executives not to sense a winner when the trade journals—whose raison d'être was to advise exhibitors on the likely popular appeal of films—were so upbeat in their assessment of this one's commercial prospects (figure 5.1). The *Daily Cinema* told exhibitors that it

A BIZARRE COMEDY MELODRAMA

FIGURE 5.1 The UK quad poster for *Dr. No* boldly declared that it would be "The First James Bond Film." Courtesy of Shawshots/Alamy.

offered a "highly potent box office brew of sex, sadism, skullduggery and snob values, expertly blended under Jamaican skies . . . It just can't fail to make a fortune and, if its amoral brutality bothers you, you can cry all the way to the bank."[7] *Kine Weekly* similarly thought it an "exuberant, lushly mounted British 'blood and thunder,' adapted from Ian Fleming's popular novel and finely photographed in Technicolor . . . The upshot is disarmingly ingenuous, yet highly polished, 'Big Boys' Own Paper.' Capital British box-office hokum."[8] And *Variety*, which, unlike the other American trade papers, would review British films following their London trade show, reported that *Dr. No* was "to be the first of a series which should be both popular and profitable ... As a screen hero, James Bond is clearly here to stay. He will win no Oscars but a heck of a lot of enthusiastic followers."⁹

Most of the reviews of *Dr. No* from the national press were also positive. The popular press pointed toward it being an audience-pleasing film, though there was a disinclination to take it too seriously. Dick Richards (*Daily Mirror*) summed up this view in calling it a "joyful piece of hammed-up hokum."¹⁰ Derek Hill (*Topic*) called it "a glossy and vigorously handled adventure thriller destined to make a fortune."¹¹ For Alexander Walker (*Evening Standard*): "By putting their tongues often enough in their cheeks, the producers manage to turn Ian Fleming's often unsavoury plot ingredients into what you could call sadism for the family ... [This] thriller is content if it makes your mind boggle—which it does, with the powerful help of Ken Adam's sets—and then leaves you smiling tolerantly at your own naivete."¹² Margaret Hinxman (*Daily Herald*) thought that it revealed "a totally unexpected sophistication that catches the tone of the Fleming novels" and that "it moves sure-footedly through a gruesome, cloud-cuckoo world where murder is a refined art, sexual provocation a formality and international power politics a game played callously by thugs."¹³ Most critics found that Sean Connery made an excellent Bond, though several reviewers, evidently unable to place his soft Edinburgh burr, thought he was Irish. Leonard Mosley (*Daily Express*), for instance, averred that "*Dr. No* is fun all the way, and even the sex is harmless. Bond is played by a virile-looking young Irishman named Sean Connery with a debonair, deadpan élan that matches the pace of the story."¹⁴ And Cecil Wilson (*Daily Mail*) said that "the film has an engaging air of chuckling at its own absurdities . . . Sean Connery, with his leathery face, Tarzan torso, dark brown Irish voice and arrogant disregard for the deadliest dangers, bestrides a world mid-way between pre-war Bulldog Drummond and post-war science extravaganza."¹⁵

Dr. No also found admirers among the ranks of the critics for the quality press who were usually more inclined toward social realism and literary adaptations than sensational melodrama or fantasy adventure. For Dilys Powell (*The Sunday Times*):

> Efficiency: perhaps that doesn't sound high praise for *Dr. No*, but I mean it as high. The first of the James Bond films (I trust it will not be the last) has the air of knowing exactly what it is up to, and that has not been common in British thrillers since the day Hitchcock took himself off to Hollywood. The jokes (one of them, a beauty, has been buzzing around London all the week) are tossed away with exactly the right carelessness. The excitements have a right little skin-crawling effect, but they aren't over-emphasised; the hair's-breadth escape from the ambush is handled with the nonchalance proper to agent 007; all in the day's work, now for the next, please.¹⁶

Angela Milne (*Punch*) indicated a similar response to the film:

> "Pleasant" is the last word I expected to choose for the film of one of Ian Fleming's James Bond novels. But *Dr. No* has

managed to cut out the nastiness, the sadism which in this novel at any rate (it happens to be the first and last Bond I ever read) so carefully unbalances plot and human interest. Here the story's the thing: a ridiculous thing of Secret Agent versus Master Mind but the rewriting and direction ensure that you don't take anything very seriously—not even the nuclear reactor to-do which has taken the place of those very explicit tortures.[17]

David Robinson (*The Financial Times*) thought that "the whole thing has the carefree fantasy of a "thirties sub-Hitchcock thriller with an amiable confusion of H-Bomb plots, green-lit Gothick dungeons, and Caligari dens presided over by a Mabuse master-criminal of Oriental origins. Terence Fisher [*sic*] directs with his accustomed efficiency and weakness for interior decoration."[18] (Robinson had confused Terence Young with the director of Hammer horror films such as *The Curse of Frankenstein*, *Dracula*, and *The Mummy*: Terence Fisher was a visual stylist whose films were notable for their richly detailed mise-en-scène and set dressings [figure 5.2].) For Penelope Gilliat (*The Observer*), "*Dr. No* is full of submerged self-parody, and I think it would be as wrong to take it solemnly as it would be to worry that Sherlock Holmes's beastliness to Dr. Watson encourages intellectual arrogance or the taking of cocaine."[19] And John Coleman (*The New Statesman*) felt that "the criminal, carnal antics of James Bond were obviously just what the director ordered, but it must be said that the director, Terence Young, has known how to temper them for mass consumption . . . If

A BIZARRE COMEDY MELODRAMA

FIGURE 5.2 "Caligari dens presided over by a Mabuse master-criminal of Oriental origin." *Dr. No* (Danjaq LLC/United Artists Corporation, 1962).

violent reveries are the style, this may well be the first in a chain of comparatively innocuous Bonded goods: no one could take these antics seriously."[20]

Some reviewers averred that *Dr. No* did not capture the true spirit of Ian Fleming. *The Guardian*'s unnamed film critic felt that it

> does not tell the best of the cool, sadistical, documentary and sexy adventures of this modern British master-spy . . . This is partly because Sean Connery, though he very nearly looks right, sounds all wrong (with his slightly Irish, slightly American accent) and partly because there seems to be no time on the screen for all those meticulous details of human

routine which are so important a part of the Fleming formula.²¹

The Times similarly thought that Connery had

a faint Irish-American look and sound, which somehow spoils the image ... For the rest, *Dr. No* is a carefully, expertly made ("manufactured" would perhaps be the better word) exercise in violence and sadism so shaped that the audience is conditioned into believing that it is witnessing the last word in sophisticated thrills decked out with ever more sophisticated trimmings of sex.²²

The specialist film press was less enthusiastic than the national critics. Peter John Dyer (*Monthly Film Bulletin*) found it wanting in comparison to other film thrillers:

Once the cluttered preliminaries are out of the way—for instance the film is obviously destined to be the first of a James Bond series, so M must be glimpsed at his London desk—the story proceeds in traditional thick-ear fashion from vamps and violent death to the fitting grandeur of a violent holocaust ... And yet strangely enough excitement, and humour, and the glamour of corruption are all rather lacking. Just as, say, *The 1,000 Eyes of Dr. Mabuse* seemed to wander anachronistically through the motions of once splendid (and why not still?) devices that Lang no longer retained much apparent faith in, *Dr. No* misses the genuine, sybaritic relish of Fleming's novels, and the narrative invention of even second-rate Hitchcock.[23]

By contrast, Penelope Houston (*Sight & Sound*) found that the film was only too close to the snobbery-with-violence ethos of the book:

> All the accusations made against Ian Fleming's novels (the sadism; the snobbism; the fantasies of master criminals with their recherché torture chambers and silken splendours) can now be repeated, as they no doubt will be, against the film ... *Dr. No* makes almost no appeal that is not to everyone's worst instincts: innocent blood and thunder have been left some way behind ... One really excellent joke—revealing the whereabouts of the National Gallery's missing Goya—almost tempts one to let this reprehensible (but admittedly watchable) film off with a caution.[24]

Tony Rose (*Amateur Cine World*) particularly admired the title graphics: "Among the chorus of shocked, amused and grudging admiration accorded to the film version of Ian Fleming's *Dr. No*, I failed to catch any reference to the opening titles. Which is rather surprising because the titles ... are eye catching to say the least and quite an entertainment in themselves."[25]

There were some more negative reviews. These fell into two distinct groups. Some critics simply found *Dr. No* too risible to take seriously and resorted to the tried-and-trusted tactic of ridicule. Ernest Betts (*The People*) was disappointed: "I expected something better than this. We get a clumsy script which boobs in your face and some hammy situations that send the thrills skidding for laughs . . . Sean Connery's James Bond is a good effort, wasted on a fantastically silly story."[26] Ian Cameron (*The Spectator*) was dismissive in the extreme: "*Dr. No*: no, no. Too inept to be as pernicious as it might have been. Costly gloss flawed by insidious economy on girls. Superannuated Rank starlet tries to act sexy. Grotesque."[27] The other group were critics who did take it all very seriously indeed and expressed their distaste for a film that sought to turn violence and sadism into popular entertainment. Nina Hibbin (*Daily Worker*)—the official mouthpiece of the Communist Party of Great Britain—was particularly outspoken: "I wouldn't have minded if this fantastic yarn of an underwater nuclear reactor run by a power-mad scientist had simply been a load of harmless hokum. Trouble is, it is vicious hokum skilfully designed to appeal to the filmgoer's basest feelings . . . Worse than brutal, it is a brutalised film."[28] Thomas Wiseman (*Sunday Express*) observed that the film's protagonist acts "with a surprising disregard for the normal movie ethics which lay down that a hero must behave like a hero . . . And I find it disturbing that we should be offered as a hero—as someone we are supposed to admire—a man whose methods and morals are indistinguishable from those of the villain."[29] And Richard Whitehall (*Films and Filming*) called it "the headiest box-office concoction of sex and sadism ever brewed in a British studio" and questioned why it had been released with an "A" certificate (permitting under-sixteens to see it when accompanied by a parent or guardian) rather than the more restrictive "X" certificate: "This is one of the X'iest films imaginable, a monstrously overblown sex fantasy of nightmarish proportions. Morally the film is indefensible with its lavishly detailed excesses, the contemporary equivalent of watching Christians being fed to the lions, and yet its lascivious dedication to violence is a genuine hypnotic." Whitehall saw *Dr. No* in the same tradition as the Mickey Spillane/Mike Hammer films of the 1950s—*I, the Jury* (1953) and *Kiss Me Deadly* (1955)—and compared it to Michael Powell's controversial *Peeping Tom* (1960). He highlighted the scene where Bond kills Professor Dent ("At one point Bond nonchalantly fires half a dozen shots into the *back* of a helpless opponent") and labelled *Dr. No* "the perfect film for a sado-masochistic society."[30]

However, *Dr. No* was the sort of film that proved to be criticproof. It was very soon apparent that it was a major hit with the cinemagoing public. A week after its première, the *Kine* reported: "A few carping critics gave *Dr. No* both barrels, but, no matter, the cash customers have been rolling up in their thousands ever since it opened on Friday . . . *Dr. No* is playing five times on weekdays and twice on Sundays. What's more, the British thriller got off to a terrific flyer on its current Market release."[31] Monty Morton, head of UA's British distribution arm, told the trade shortly after *Dr. No*'s release that "we have another sensational winner on our hands."[32] This was confirmed by the *Kine* at the beginning of November: "*Dr. No* finished its first London run in a blaze of glory, but it's not just sitting on its huge pot of gold . . . The Ian Fleming thriller started at the top and, surprising as it may seem, rapidly built up. The sky's definitely its limit."[33] In his annual roundup of box office "winners," *Kine*'s "Josh" Billings ranked *Dr. No* second among the general releases narrowly behind the Cliff Richard musical *The Young*

Ones (which had been released a full eight months before *Dr. No* and so had had a longer run in cinemas): "The second biggest winner is *Dr. No*, a bizarre comedy melodrama based on Ian Fleming's best-seller character James Bond. It took a stack of money at the London Pavilion and throughout the London suburbs and is still earning large sums around the provinces."[34] *Films and Filming* had *Dr. No* ahead of *The Young Ones* and behind only *The Guns of Navarone*, which had been shown as a "hard-ticket special" in 1961 before a general release in 1962.[35] (There are no published records for box-office receipts of individual films for the United Kingdom at this time: the press based its ranking of "winners" on information provided by distributors but did not reveal the actual returns.)

Terence Young believed that the picture's success was intimately tied to its historical moment. He thought that *Dr. No* was "the most perfectly timed film ever made . . . I think we arrived [in] not only the right year, but the right week of the right month of the right year."[36] The coincidence of the film's UK release coinciding with the Cuban Missile Crisis—the revelation that the Soviet Union had stationed ballistic missiles in Cuba capable of reaching the American mainland—imparted a degree of topicality that the producers could not have intended but could hardly pass unnoticed by audiences. As J. Hoberman observes: "*Dr. No* was not the most extravagant of Bond novels, but it was surely the most timely in its concern with a malevolent island despot and secret missile base in the Caribbean."[37]

The release of *Dr. No* also coincided with changes in British film culture. Here is Young again: "It fitted the mood of the people, anyway in Britain. I think people were getting tired of the realistic school, the kitchen sinks and all those abortions."[38] The "realistic school" to which Young refers was the British new wave, a cycle of films between 1959 and 1963—including *Look Back in Anger* (1959), *Room at the Top* (1959), *Saturday Night and Sunday Morning* (1960), *A Taste of Honey* (1961), *A Kind of Loving* (1962), *The Loneliness of the Long Distance Runner* (1962), *Billy Liar* (1963), and *This Sporting Life* (1963)—characterized by their adult content, their narrative focus on working-class protagonists, their stark black-and-white cinematography, and above all their social realism.[39] The new wave films were well received by critics, and some, notably *Room at the Top* and *Saturday Night and Sunday Morning*, were also successful at the box office. However, within a few years there was a sense that the movement had run its course. As the London correspondent of the US trade paper *Boxoffice* observed in April 1963: "The year 1962 saw the end of the conventional horror and the conventional 'kitchen-sink' type of pictures. The box-office results also convinced producers against making films dealing with regional stories and loading them with provincial-speaking actors."[40]

The success of *Dr. No* also needs to be seen in the context of longer-term shifts in cinemagoing, which ceased to be a regular social habit and became more of an occasional event. Cinema attendances in Britain had been in decline since their peak in the mid-1940s, but in the late 1950s this drop-off had become precipitous. In 1955, annual cinema attendances stood at 1,181,765,000 and the gross box-office takings at Britain's 4,087 cinemas amounted to over £105 million. However, by 1962, annual cinema attendances had fallen to 394,963,000, a third of the level they had been only seven years before, over two thousand cinemas had closed, and total gross takings had dropped to a little short of £57 million.[41] The decline in cinemagoing particularly affected the regular, habitual patrons who comprised around a third of the total audience. While social historians now attribute it to a range of factors, including changing demographics and increasing levels of disposable income among the working classes, who traditionally had been the most frequent cinemagoers, the film industry pointed the finger at one cause: television. There was certainly a correlation between the decline in cinemagoing and the rise of television: in 1955—the year that saw the launch of the Independent Television network in Britain—4,503,766 television licenses were issued. This had increased to 11,833,712 by 1962.[42] The industry's reasoning (as it had been in the United States) was that it needed to offer a kind of entertainment that television could not, and to provide more "event" pictures rather than routine fare in order to attract the occasional cinemagoers who still frequented their local Odeon or ABC.

There is some anecdotal evidence of the responses of ordinary cinemagoers to *Dr. No*, suggesting that it appealed to a wide age range. Alan Dent (*The Illustrated London News*) reported that "a packed teatime audience revelled in *Dr. No* and I found myself sitting—staidly—between a young woman, who fidgeted with giddy rapture throughout, and an elderly one who was so overwhelmed by the hero's more breathtaking escapades that she frequently buried her face in her hands through decorous terror."[43] The *Daily Cinema* published on its front page a letter to "The Directors, Pinewood Film Studios" from a woman in Chorlton-cum-Hardy, Manchester: "As a grandmother of a family we want to *THANK YOU* for that marvellous thriller *Dr. No*. Just shows you what the *British* film Industry can do. *Everything perfect* / ACTING / COLOUR / MARVELOUS SETS / and background music. *MORE PLEASE*. Our local cinema was crammed full. Never seen anything like it since before the War."[44] The testimony of full cinemas would suggest that *Dr. No* was one of those "event" pictures that drew occasional (and sometimes older) cinemagoers.

A further indication of the picture's success was the impact on sales of the book. The UK paperback edition of *Dr. No* had sold 85,000 copies in 1961; this rose to 232,000 in 1962, 437,000 in 1963, and 530,000 in 1964.[45] (A similar pattern occurred with all the early films, which were reissued with film tie-in covers. *From Russia with Love* sold 145,000 copies in 1962, rising to 642,000 in 1963 and 600,000 in 1964. *Goldfinger* sold 429,000 copies in 1963 and 964,000 copies in 1964.) Fleming was no doubt very satisfied with the increased sales, as well as his profit share in the film. It was after the release of *Dr. No* that he told readers of *Books and Bookmen*: "You don't make a great deal of money from royalties and translation rights and so forth . . . but if you sell the serial rights and film rights, you do very well."[46] In public, Fleming was diplomatic about his view of the film, telling the press: "Those who've read the book are likely to be disappointed, but those who haven't will find it a wonderful movie. Audiences laugh in all the right places."[47]

Dr. No was not shown to the trade in the United States until March 1963. The trade reviews were just as enthusiastic as they had been in Britain. The *Hollywood Reporter* pronounced it "a high-powered spy melodrama that crackles with intrigue and suspense and sizzles with romance ... *Dr. No* is a perfect picture of its special kind, and exactly fits that often cited but generally misunderstood category 'pure entertainment.' It should be a highly popular and profitable attraction."[48] *Film Daily* concurred: "Now here's a thriller with style, freshness and imagination ... It is sure to bring in strong box office returns ... *Dr. No* is an auspicious beginning of what looks like a thrilling series."[49] The *Independent Exhibitors' Film Bulletin* thought it "hell-bent-for-excitement from start to finish ... Already a powerful moneymaker in England, this United Artists release looks to repeat its boxoffice success in this country, because it's the kind of film guaranteed to generate word-of-mouth from the high-brows to the masses and it lends itself to showmanship."[50] The *Motion Picture Herald* predicted there would be "a wide, waiting and ready audience for the first of the films based on the James Bond stories ... There is every reason to suppose, and expect, that Harry Saltzman and Albert R. Broccoli, the producers, have here the first of what very well could be the most successful series of films of its kind since the happy days of the Charlie Chan pictures or the Thin Man films."[51] And *Boxoffice* liked its "delightfully tongue-in-cheek style" and predicted that "the first Ian Fleming novel to reach the screen has its ready-made audience of paperback readers to insure [*sic*] strong boxoffice."[52]

Critics from the major newspapers also welcomed *Dr. No*. Bosley Crowther, who had acted as arbiter of American cinephile tastes for the *New York Times* since 1940, pronounced it a "lively, amusing picture ... [that] is not to be taken seriously as realistic fiction or even art ... It is strictly a tinseled action-thriller, spiked with a mystery of a sort. And, if you are clever, you will see it as a spoof of science-fiction and sex."[53] Richard L. Coe (*Washington Post*) looked forward to a successful series: "From start to finish, *Dr. No* is a glittering, amusing stiletto in the heart of boredom . . . If the inevitable follow-ups are as good, we're in for a glorious decade."[54] Arthur Knight (*The Saturday Review*) believed that "it is just possible that director Terence Young had his tongue in his cheek most of the time" and that the approach "makes *Dr. No* a thoroughly enjoyable experience—for the audience participants at least." He concluded that it was "the best bad film of the year."[55] There were none of the outright hostile reviews seen in parts of the British press, though some critics again felt that *Dr. No* was simply too absurd to be taken seriously. Brandan Gill (*The New Yorker*) pronounced it "a trashy success."[56] Stanley Kaufman (*The New Republic*) was underwhelmed by a film that he felt "never decides whether it is suspense or suspense-proof."[57] And the review for *Time*, titled "Hairy Marshmallow," felt that the film was inferior to the books and would disappoint their readers, asking rhetorically: "Is it possible to make a good movie out of a James Bond thriller? Fleming fans probably won't take *No* for an answer."[58]

Another one of the myths about *Dr. No* is that United Artists did not recognize the film's potential in the US market and so afforded it a low-profile release. According to Cubby Broccoli: "[The] geniuses who made the decisions at the time liked the picture but lacked the courage to go with their hunches . . . The result was that, instead of opening the picture in key places like New York or Chicago, they opened at drive-in cinemas in

Oklahoma and Texas."[59] In fact, United Artists planned and executed a carefully coordinated release strategy for *Dr. No* in America. This started during the film's production with a press junket to Jamaica for around sixty journalists, who were flown out on the inaugural Pan-Am flight from New York to Kingston.[60] Beginning in early 1963, there was a major prerelease campaign across the United States to build up Sean Connery: in March—shortly before the commencement of principal photography on *From Russia with Love*—Connery and Terence Young visited New York, Chicago, Los Angeles, and San Francisco. The tour included a national convention of independent exhibitors in Kansas City, where "*Dr. No* is the conference's 'project film' and theatremen will meet Connery, who will be accompanied by three lovely models, clad in bikinis and other revealing costumes." According to UA vice-president Fred Goldberg: "We consider the James Bond thrillers the hottest piece of film in some years."[61]

United Artists' promotional strategy for *Dr. No* was alert to the film's exploitation value and its potential for product tie-ins. The US press book emphasized the Fleming books, now published in America by Signet—claiming that *Dr. No* was "currently the most popular of this famous author's Secret Agent 007 stories"—and the soundtrack LP released by United Artists Records. Much was made of "Bondmanship," and photographs of a bikini-clad Ursula Andress were included with the press pack. It was the producers' idea to approach publisher Dick Kravitz with a view to producing an adaptation of *Dr. No* for *Classics Illustrated*.[62] This was a comic book launched in 1942 that had originally specialized in adaptations of literary classics by authors including Alexandre Dumas and Sir Walter Scott, but more recently had branched out into versions of popular movies. A *Dr. No* comic book was published under this imprint in the United Kingdom and by DC Comics as part of its *Showcase* series in the United States. The latter hit newsstands in January 1963, five months before the release of the film.

Dr. No opened at 450 locations across the United States, including Dallas, Denver, Kansas City, Minneapolis, and St. Louis, in early May 1963. *Variety* reported: "UA has been going high on the promotion angles and wants to rush to market while the property is supposedly 'hot.'"[63] A month later, it opened in New York as a "première showcase" release, where it set a record for the "first four-day gross . . . UA has a tremendous winner."[64] It "tallied a hefty $477,743" in a three-week run at select theaters, including the Astor on Broadway, and was held over for a fourth week at six of the showcase sites. Other cities followed the same strategy. On June 26, *Variety* reported: "The picture has been registering well in various situations around the country and overseas. In the Gotham area, *Dr. No* opens in 80 circuit houses and indie theaters today . . . Big biz being tallied by *Dr. No* is heartening indeed to UA execs who are planning a series of six pix based on Fleming James Bond books."[65] More qualitative evidence of the film's reception can be gleaned from *Boxoffice*, which included a regular column ("The Exhibitor Has His Say") featuring reports from independent exhibitors across the country. These point toward a generally positive response to *Dr. No* in the "sticks." It went down well with patrons of the Crescent Theatre in Jasonville, Indiana

("A better-than-average crime drama, with beautiful color. It was talked about very much"), the Jackson Theatre in Flomaton, Alaska ("An excellent picture crammed with top-notch entertainment, beautiful color and perfect cast"), the Comfrey Theatre in Comfrey, Minnesota ("This was another well-liked production that will drive and build business") and the New Theatre in England, Arkansas ("A new star in a different sort of picture, which did fine business in a saturation booking"), though it underperformed at the Fiesta Theatre in Gillette, Wyoming ("My people ate it up. Business only fair due to circus in town").[66]

By the end of 1963, *Dr. No* had earned $2.1 million in rentals in North America and was projected to reach $2.4 million. At the time, $1 million was regarded as the yardstick for a "big" rental. Even so, *Dr. No* was only number forty-four in the box-office ranking for the year, and a long way behind *Cleopatra* ($15.7 million), *The Longest Day* ($12.8 million), *Lawrence of Arabia* ($9 million) and *How the West Was Won* ($8 million), although those films had been released as roadshows at higher ticket prices in advance of their general release. The rentals of *Dr. No* were on a par with films such as *Jason and the Argonauts* ($2.4 million), *Sodom and Gomorrah* ($2.1 million) and *Captain Sindbad* ($2 million).[67] This would point toward *Dr. No* being a successful release in America, but not exceptionally so. However, it needs to be borne in mind that *Dr. No* was offered to exhibitors on especially favorable terms: 30 percent to the distributor with 70 percent retained by the exhibitor. A rental of $2.1 million at 30 percent would suggest a total box-office gross of around $7 million. It is possible, therefore, that *Dr. No* was more successful at the box office in comparison to other films with a return more favorable to the distributor.

The Bond films ran counter to the usual pattern that sequels perform less well at the box office. *From Russia with Love*, released in the United States and Canada in April 1964, returned rentals of $3,849,000 by the year's end, placing it sixteenth at the box office.[68] However, it was *Goldfinger*, released in December 1964, that really marked the breakthrough for Bond at the US box office: it returned $19.7 million by the end of 1965 (coming in third overall behind *Mary Poppins* and *The Sound of Music*).[69] Its significantly higher rentals were due in some measure to the distributor's taking a higher percentage of the box office, up to 90 percent for the first run, though there were some variations. *Variety* reported: "This kind of business has inevitably had its effect on the terms which UA has been able to get. While all the key dates were on 90–10 deals, reports [are] coming in from the field that many of the 60–40 dates are being settled at 70–30. In some cases, the biz has been so phenomenal that the theaters have 'volunteered' to up the distrib's share to 70%."[70]

The success of *Goldfinger* prompted United Artists to reissue the first two Bond pictures on a double bill in spring 1965 ("James Bond is back . . . to back"). The reissue was offered on a 50 percent split and returned $7 million to the distributor: this was more than the combined total of the original release of the two films, which performed better "in their second run at the wickets."[71] *Variety* reported that "the oldie combo racked up a sensational $611,321 in six days of first week in Showcase" in New York.[72] *Boxoffice* reported that the *Dr. No–From Russia with*

A BIZARRE COMEDY MELODRAMA

Love double bill grossed four times the house average at the Royal Theatre in San Francisco.[73] And the manager of the Fiesta Drive-In in Winter, Texas, called it "the best double bill we have had in a long time."[74] Another double-bill reissue—this time of *Dr. No* and *Goldfinger*—followed in the fall of 1966. This time UA took a "hefty" 60 percent of the box office. The manager of the Odeon Theatre, Ontario, reported "another Bond-buster double. They were lined up again for another week . . . It seems these are not milked yet."[75] By the end of 1966, *Dr. No*'s North American rentals amounted to $4.6 million. Its two reissues had more than doubled its first-run return. This was an unprecedented achievement even allowing for the higher renters' percentages of the reissues.

As in Britain, the success of the Bond pictures in the United States needs to be understood in relation to changes in the film industry and film culture. Cinema attendance was in long-term decline—average weekly attendances had fallen from 90 million in 1946 to 41.9 million by 1963—and total US box-office grosses had fallen from $2.4 billion a year to $852 million over the same period.[76] The US film industry had responded by adopting the blockbuster strategy: the production of expensive films that would be released on a selective roadshow basis before going on general release. John Sedgwick has analyzed box-office trends in the United States between 1946 and 1965 and demonstrates "that film audiences became more discriminating over this period. The secular decline in filmgoing as a leisure activity resulted in increasing numbers becoming only *occasional* visitors to the cinema, who were attracted by particular vertically differentiated high-profile production."[77] However, the Bond pictures represented a different sort of release strategy: UA adopted a wide-market release to maximize publicity. *Goldfinger*, for example, opened in forty cities in North America and with 1,100 prints worldwide. In America it "racked up $10,374,807 in its first 14 weeks"—it had already recouped its production cost in Britain—and "has a good chance of becoming the biggest-grossing non-roadshow film in domestic distribution history."[78]

The success of the Bond films in the United States was due to more than just canny marketing and a saturation release. Paul Monaco has argued that "the Bond movies offered Hollywood a model for a slick entertainment package that deftly skirted what was left of Hollywood's disintegrating Production Code."[79] The authority of the Production Code Administration—already challenged by auteur filmmakers such as Alfred Hitchcock, Otto Preminger, and Billy Wilder—was waning by the 1960s. In Britain, it was the violence of the Bond pictures that seems to have bothered the censors; in the United States, it was their sexual content.[80] *Variety* suggested that the Bond films tested the boundaries of what was regarded as acceptable for younger (especially teenaged) audiences in the 1960s:

> Take, for this instance, another example from the United Artists catalog—the James Bond pictures. They are well-made, colorful, exciting entries with, as is evident from their success at the boxoffice, appeal to audiences of all ages. And it is estimated that [a] large segment of that audience has been teenagers, some of them seeing their favourite 007 adventure three or four times. With nude sequences removed from US prints, none of those pictures has received

a "condemned" rating [from the Catholic Legion of Decency], and none has run too far afoul of the specific taboos in the old code.

Yet the Bond films, however light-hearted their treatment, are seen by some as unrelieved exercises in violence, and illicit sex is one of 007's strong points. For some observers, these entertainments fit well within the category of pictures that, again quoting [Motion Picture Producers' Association president Jack] Valenti, contain "subjects and treatments that parents ought not to display for their children." UA might be considerably upset if it felt that teenagers would be taglined away from the ticket windows, but if the raison d'etre of the proposed new code is to "inform parents," won't Bond and his imitators (*Our Man Flint, The Silencers*) require a "mature audiences" tag?[81]

The context for this article was the proposed reform of the Production Code to a new ratings system that would classify films as suitable for "General," "Mature," or "Restricted" audiences. While the Bond pictures themselves were not responsible for bringing about this change, they can be seen as part of a trend during the 1960s toward the inclusion of a more generous allowance of sex and violence in popular cinema that would pave the way for films such as *Bonnie and Clyde* (1967), *Barbarella* (1968), and *The Wild Bunch* (1969).

Dr. No eventually returned total rentals of $22.1 million worldwide: $6.4 million came from North America and $15.7 million from the rest of the world.[82] The variable renters' percentages for domestic reissues, let alone the rest of the world, make it difficult to estimate the film's total box-office gross. Most sources suggest it was probably around $60 million worldwide.[83] *Dr. No* had earned 71 percent of its rental income outside North America. This set the pattern for later Bond pictures, which have usually earned between two-thirds and three-quarters of their revenues from the international market. *Dr. No* seems to have performed particularly well in Europe; this very likely influenced the choice of the "European" themed *From Russia with Love* as the second Bond picture. Ironically it did not reach Jamaica until a year after its UK release. It had been suggested that the Western Hemisphere première of *Dr. No* might take place in Kingston—Harry Saltzman had been keen on this idea—though eventually it was held in Nassau in the Bahamas.[84] It finally opened in Kingston in September 1963 and was evidently a popular success: the *Sunday Gleaner* reported in November 1964 that "the hardy *Dr. No* is still showing at city cinemas."[85]

The commercial potential of the Bond films on reissue meant that they were held back from television for rather longer than usual. In 1972, the ABC network in the United States paid an estimated $17.5 million for three television screenings of the first seven Bond pictures (*Dr. No* to *Diamonds Are Forever*): *Variety* reported that "the terms are unprecedented for a seven-picture buy and it bespeaks ABC's faith in the blockbuster value of the Bond series over numerous exposures."[86] However, it was *Goldfinger* rather than *Dr. No* that became the first Bond film shown on US television, on September 17, 1972. The first TV screening of *Dr. No* in the United States was over two years later, on November 10, 1974. In early 1974, the British press reported that ITV had paid £850,000 for two screenings of each of the first six Bond films. The deal was subsequently pushed back by a year following protests from cinema exhibitors.[87] The UK television première of *Dr. No* was on October 28, 1975: it was shown across the ITV network (except in Northern Ireland) and was seen by 10.5 million households, representing an estimated 27 million viewers.[88] The Bond films regularly attracted record audiences in Britain in the late 1970s and early 1980s, with the television première of each film as much of an "event" as its cinema release. By the time that *Dr. No* received its third screening on Christmas Day of 1981, the Bond films had become part of the cultural landscape of British television as well as British cinema.

Chapter Six

I'M JUST LOOKING

IT IS TIME now to turn our attention to the film itself. What does an analysis of *Dr. No* reveal about the film and its place in film culture? This is separate from the question of whether *Dr. No* is a good or a bad film from a technical or artistic point of view. Certainly it is an exemplary case study of the complex and often contradictory relationship between the formal properties and ideological processes of popular cinema. On the one hand, *Dr. No* may be placed within a modernizing trend in British cinema of the 1960s: it exemplifies a decisive shift away from the moribund class-bound nature of British films of the previous decade and marks the emergence of a more expressive visual style where the realist aesthetic was still a dominant influence. On the other hand, the film has been seen as retrograde and even reactionary in its cultural politics: it perpetuates an archetype of white imperialist masculinity and its gender and (especially) racial politics are ideologically problematic at the very least. Indeed, it may be argued that the distinctive qualities of *Dr. No*—the characteristics that made it stand out at the time—arise from these contradictory ideological and formal impulses.

The opening sequence immediately establishes its difference from the stylistic norms of British cinema. The script had envisioned a fairly standard title sequence with the credits superimposed over a montage of the three "blind" beggars making their way through Kingston, ending with their arrival outside Queen's Club.[1] Instead, the film eschews naturalistic exposition for abstraction and symbolism. It begins with a series of overlapping white computer dots tracking from left to right across the screen—pausing in the middle of the screen for the producers' names ("Harry Saltzman & Albert R. Broccoli present...")—while a high-pitched electronic noise is heard on the soundtrack. The last dot expands (fast xylophone scale) to become the inner circle of a gun barrel: this is denoted by the rifling effects around the edges of the frame. The barrel tracks left, following the figure of "Bond," who suddenly jumps and fires a pistol at the camera (figure 6.1). At this point, a red wash cascades down the screen and the "James Bond Theme" played on electric guitar bursts onto the soundtrack.

The gun barrel was designed by Maurice Binder, a former art director who had created the innovative title graphics for films including *Indiscreet* (1958), *The Mouse That Roared* (1959), *The Grass Is Greener* (1960) and *Road to Hong Kong* (1962). Binder explained how he achieved the effect in an interview for *Amateur Movie-Maker* shortly after *Dr. No*'s release:

I'M JUST LOOKING

FIGURE 6.1 Maurice Binder's gun barrel motif foregrounds "cinema's inherent scopic regime." "Bond" is played by stuntman Bob Simmons. *Dr. No* (Danjaq LLC/United Artists Corporation, 1962).

I started the design with elements from computers and electronic sounds which eventually worked into the James Bond figure seen through the barrel of a gun. Incidentally, I find that drawing circles is a bore so for the computer dots, I used ordinary gummed labels from a stationery store (an idea that amateurs might care to adopt) and these were animated by my colleague Trevor Bond . . . The gun barrel was a still photograph taken by Saunders Studios and the only way we could get sufficient depth of field for this with the gun barrel right up against the lens of the camera was to put a hole pierced in a sheet of cardboard. This was then combined by double printing with a normal live action shot of Bond, the edges of which had been matted out to leave only the centre hole.[2]

A variant of the same sequence was featured in all but one of the subsequent Bond films made by Eon Productions. Binder's account of the low-tech ingenuity used to create the effect has become part of Bond history—but it is also more than that. The opening of *Dr. No* links the film to experimental cinema and the avant-garde through its insistence upon optical subjectivity and its employment of non-naturalistic sound effects. Binder's work employs some of the techniques, including still photography and double printing, characteristic of what became known as "Structural-Materialist" film-making in the 1960s.[3]

The gun barrel is an "impossible" point-of-view shot: it is the equivalent of effects such as extreme overhead shots or shots from behind a fireplace that serve to draw attention to the position of the camera and place the spectator in a privileged position in relation to characters in the film. Jan-Christopher Horak argues that the sequence turns around "cinema's inherent scopic regime," writing: "The audience as voyeur—the circular view is surrounded by what looks to be a shutter—sees without being seen but is also placed in the position of a potential Bond assassin. However, when James Bond turns, pulls his gun, and fires at the audience, the tables are turned . . . The audience becomes the victim of violence, rather than the potential perpetrator."[4] The gun barrel also links *Dr. No* to the "cinema of attractions" that prevailed during the early years of the medium before narrative filmmaking established its dominance. In particular, it recalls the moment when an outlaw fires a revolver at the camera in Edwin S. Porter's *The Great Train Robbery* (1903). This was a stand-alone shot disconnected from the narrative that exhibitors could place either at the beginning or the end of the film.[5]

In later Bond films, the gun barrel would dissolve into a sequence before the main titles, but in *Dr. No* it segues directly into the credits, which again suggests links to traditions of experimental filmmaking. The first part of the title sequence is a "colourful animated-dot spectacular" in which multicolored dots form both symmetrical and asymmetrical patterns: the exception to the dots is the "007" on a red film strip that appears next to Sean Connery's name.[6] This segues into silhouettes of dancers (red, orange, lavender, and green against a black background) as the "James Bond Theme" gives way to calypso music, concluding with a jaunty rendition of "Three Blind Mice" as the silhouettes dissolve to the "blind" beggars in Kingston. In particular, the titles of *Dr. No* recall the short films of New Zealand–born animator Len Lye for the GPO Film Unit in the 1930s, such as *A Colour Box* (1935) and *Rainbow Dance* (1936).[7] But they also suggest a more contemporary influence: the Pop Art movement—emerging from the late 1950s in the work of artists such as Richard Hamilton in Britain and Andy Warhol in the United States—also favored bold colors and images detached from their original contexts. The Museum of Modern Art in New York coincidentally held its first exhibition of Pop Art in December 1962.[8]

The dazzling titles of *Dr. No* represent a radical departure from the visual style of British films of the previous decade. With some notable exceptions, such as the early Hammer horror films, British cinema of the 1950s had tended toward a sober monochrome realism that shied away from visual excess and extreme stylization. *Dr. No* was signaling its difference from this tradition; this marked the beginning of a shift toward colorful fantasy in the 1960s. Its title design would also influence those of television spy/adventure series such as ITC's *The Saint* (1962–1968) and *Man in a Suitcase* (1967–1968) and NBC's *I Spy* (1965–1968) which also feature color silhouettes against black backgrounds. David Buxton has highlighted the association between the spy/secret agent genre in the 1960s—including the comic strip and film of *Modesty Blaise* (1966)—and the cultural moment of "pop":

> One of the strengths of pop was its ability to take form in several different media: films, television series, novels and, last but not least, comics. Some pop texts like James Bond, *The Ipcress File*, and *Modesty Blaise* existed in two or three media forms . . . As well as being an agent of national or imperial interests, the spy brings into play a new gaze on the world of objects: he is, to use the expression of [Michael] Denning, "licensed to look" and is also, in turn, the object of the gaze of others, a perfect, "cool" surface unruffled by uncontrolled emotion or ambition.[9]

The spy film was particularly amenable to a "pop" aesthetic on account of its preoccupation with material culture and consumer artefacts. Ian Fleming's novels had prefigured the aesthetic of product placement that would assume even greater prominence in the Bond films as they went on: the only conspicuously visible brands in the film of *Dr. No* are Pan-American Airways, Smirnoff vodka, and Dom Perignon champagne.

Even the most trenchant critics of the narrative politics of *Dr. No* accept that it is a tour de force of production design. Ken

Adam's sets became such a defining feature of the "look" of the Bond films that it is worth remembering he worked on only seven of them: *Dr. No, Goldfinger, Thunderball, You Only Live Twice, Diamonds Are Forever, The Spy Who Loved Me,* and *Moonraker*. Adam was an extraordinarily versatile production designer whose work ranged from the period mise-en-scène of costume pictures such as *The Trials of Oscar Wilde* (1960) and *Barry Lyndon* (1975) to the futuristic modernism of *Dr. Strangelove; or, How I Learned to Stop Worrying and Love the Bomb* (1964).[10] Adam said that he accepted the offer to design *Dr. No* because he "felt that this chaotic secret-agent plot might enable me to experiment with a new form of design."[11] He employs three distinct styles in *Dr. No* that not only demonstrate the full extent of his visual imagination but also suggest a coherent and carefully planned approach to the "look" of the film. The first style—exemplified by the elegant interior of the upscale gambling club Les Ambassadeurs and the wood-panelled furnishings and naval paintings of M's office—represents tradition and establishment values. The script provides only a brief description of Les Ambassadeurs ("A large high-ceilinged rococo room crowded with obvious café society") and nothing for M's office: Adam seems to have taken the Fleming novels as his reference point here. The second style—exemplified by Dr. No's reactor room—is best described as high modernism, emphasizing geometric angles and gleaming metallic surfaces. This style highlights the science-fictional elements of the film and provides a visual contrast with the world of London clubland depicted earlier. Even so, Adam was keen to emphasize that the set had some basis in reality: he explained that he consulted "two young scientists" from the Atomic Energy Research Establishment at Harwell, Oxfordshire, who advised him on the design of a uranium nuclear water reactor.[12]

The third style is what might be described as a form of modernist expressionism (or expressionist modernism). Adam admired the design of German Expressionist films such as *The Cabinet of Dr. Caligari* (1920) and *Dr. Mabuse, the Gambler* (1922), with their stylized theatricality and distorted perspectives, and sought to include visual references in his work. One of the most memorable sets in *Dr. No* is the "tarantula room" where Professor Dent receives his orders from the voice of the unseen Dr. No: it exemplifies a minimalist aesthetic, with sparse furnishings whose main feature is a circular grille in the roof (a motif that would become an Adam trademark) (figure 6.2a). It marks the point at which *Dr. No* switches from what has hitherto been a fairly routine procedural to something more fantastical and bizarre. By contrast, Adam's set for Dr. No's underground lair interprets the script description ("The room is high-ceilinged, about sixty feet long, but with furnishings and fittings so fantastic that it is impossible to imagine what sort of man lives here") freely to include sumptuous modern furnishings with a stone fireplace, candelabras, antiques, and stolen old masters (figure 6.2b).[13] (Adam himself painted the prop Goya based on a postcard from the National Gallery.) Here, the design locates Dr. No visually in a lineage of megalomaniacs, master criminals, mesmerists, and tyrants who populated the cinema of Weimar Germany.

The visual style of *Dr. No* therefore highlights its difference from the dominant realist aesthetic of British cinema. The

FIGURE 6.2 Ken Adam's highly stylized sets demonstrate the influence of German Expressionism. *Dr. No* (Danjaq LLC/United Artists Corporation, 1962).

contrast with the films of the British new wave—those that best represented the critically acclaimed tradition of social realism—could not be more stark: the glossy, high-contrast Technicolor cinematography of Ted Moore presents a colorful alternative to the landscapes of the back streets and canals of grim industrial towns that characterize the earlier style.[14] Like Adam, Moore would work on seven Bonds in total: he followed *Dr. No* with *From Russia with Love, Goldfinger, Thunderball, Diamonds Are Forever, Live and Let Die,* and *The Man with the Golden Gun*. Duncan Petrie considers that his "assured cinematography set the style for the Bond movies, emphasising the glamour and excitement of agent 007's world which is a combination of exotic locations, in this case Jamaica, and glossy interiors."[15]

While the "look" of *Dr. No* works to position Bond within a mode of cultural modernity, the narrative politics of the film balance both progressive and reactionary social discourses. In this context, it is useful to consider Umberto Eco's influential analysis of the politics of the Bond novels in his essay "The Narrative Structure in Fleming," first published in 1965. Eco is concerned not with the works' literary qualities, but rather how their narratives are structured around a set of ideological paradigms. He adopts the method of structuralist analysis and determines that the Bond stories rehearse a set of binary oppositions between characters (Bond/M, Bond/Villain, Bond/Woman), between ideologies (Free World/Soviet Union, Great Britain/non–Anglo Saxon countries) and between states of being (love/death, loyalty/disloyalty, excess/moderation, luxury/discomfort).[16] Eco analyzes the Bond novels through the metaphor of a game of chess where various archetypal characters all make certain predetermined moves. He concludes that the underlying similarity of the Bond books is the reason for their appeal: "The reader's pleasure consists of finding himself immersed in a game of which he knows the pieces and the rules—and perhaps the outcome—drawing pleasure simply from following the minimal variations by which the victor realises his objective."[17]

Eco identifies the "invariable scheme" of the Bond narratives as follows:

A. M moves and gives a task to Bond.
B. Villain moves and appears to Bond (perhaps in alternating forms).
C. Bond moves and gives first check to the Villain, or the Villain gives first check to Bond.
D. The Woman moves and shows herself to Bond.
E. Bond consumes Woman: possesses her or begins her seduction.
F. The Villain captures Bond (with or without Woman, or at different moments).
G. The Villain tortures Bond (with or without Woman).
H. Bond conquers the Villain (kills him, or kills his representative, or helps at their killing).
I. Bond convalescing enjoys Woman, whom he then loses.

"The scheme is invariable in the sense that all the elements are always present in every novel," Eco amplifies. "It is not imperative that the moves always be in the same sequence."[18] (In fact, this is not strictly correct. *The Spy Who Loved Me*—in which Fleming varied the formula by telling the story from the woman's point of view and where Bond makes his appearance only midway into the narrative—does not conform to this pattern: Eco dismisses it as being "quite untypical." Most of the short stories—including "Quantum of Solace," "The Hildebrand Rarity," "Octopussy," "The Property of a Lady," and "The Living Daylights"—also do not conform, while "From a View to a Kill," "For Your Eyes Only," and "Risico" do so only partially.)

Dr. No is one of the books that fits Eco's structure particularly closely, with only one significant difference: the first chapter constitutes a prologue describing the murder of John Strangways, the local Secret Service head of station in the Caribbean, and his number two, Mary Trueblood. Otherwise, a narrative map of the novel would look like this:

A. M sends Bond to Jamaica to investigate the disappearance of Strangways and Trueblood, not knowing at this time that they have been murdered. It is established that Strangways had been investigating the activities of one Dr. Julius No, who owns a guano-processing plant on an island called Crab Key.

B. Bond arrives in Jamaica and meets his ally, the Cayman Islander Quarrel (who previously appeared in *Live and Let Die*). The villain appears to Bond in the form of a female photographer who captures his picture at the airport.

C. The villain gives first check to Bond by making attempts to kill him with poisoned fruit and by putting a deadly tropical centipede in his bed.

D. Bond and Quarrel sail by night to Crab Key, where in the morning Bond meets the woman (Honeychile), who is diving for shells. After a motor launch shoots up Honeychile's canoe with a machine gun, she accompanies Bond and Quarrel in their trek across the island.

E. Bond begins the process of seducing the woman. In this section, there are also further variations on move C: Bond gives check to Dr. No by killing one of his men in the mangrove swamp; Dr. No counters and gives check to Bond when his marsh buggy kills Quarrel with a flame-thrower.

F. Dr. No's men capture Bond and Honeychile. They are taken to Dr. No's headquarters, where they are imprisoned in a luxurious "hotel." Bond and Honeychile meet Dr. No, who tells them of his background and explains his scheme to interfere with test launches of US missiles with a radio beam.

G. Dr. No tortures Bond by forcing him to navigate his way through an obstacle course laced with booby-traps in the ventilation system. At the same time, he intends to kill Honeychile by staking her in the path of carnivorous land crabs.

H. Bond evades Dr. No's traps and finds his way to the docks. He commandeers a crane and kills Dr. No by burying him under a pile of guano. He finds Honeychile (who has escaped from the crabs) and they escape from Dr. No's headquarters in the marsh buggy.

I. After sending his report to London, Bond convalesces with Honeychile.

Dr. No is therefore a particularly schematic example of the narrative structure of the Bond books insofar as it includes all the archetypal elements in a linear sequence.

We have seen how the script of *Dr. No* underwent multiple revisions that brought it progressively into closer alignment with Fleming's novel. The finished film conforms quite closely to the structure of the book, though there are some differences. The disappearance of Strangways is treated as a much more urgent matter in the film: three weeks have passed in the novel before M sends Bond to investigate, but in the film it is only a matter of hours before the agent is summoned to M's office ("We've been burning the air between here and Jamaica for the last three hours," Miss Moneypenny tells Bond). The film also suggests something about the nature of Dr. No's conspiracy in the briefing between Bond and M, whereas in the book it is not until Bond's meeting with Dr. No that this is explained. Otherwise, the film maintains the narrative structure of the book, as well as many of the same specific incidents:

A. M sends Bond to Jamaica to investigate the disappearance of Strangways and his secretary. He explains that Strangways was looking into an inquiry made by the Americans ("They've been complaining about massive interference with their Cape Canaveral rockets") and asks Bond what he knows about "toppling."

B. Bond arrives in Jamaica, where he meets his allies, Felix Leiter and Quarrel. The villain appears to Bond in the form of the imposter chauffeur "Mr. Jones" and the woman photographer.

C. The villain gives first check to Bond by attempting to kill him with a tarantula and in a road ambush. Bond gives check to the villain by uncovering his agent, Miss Taro, and killing his subordinate, Professor Dent.

D. Bond and Quarrel sail by night to Crab Key, where in the morning Bond meets the woman (Honey). After the "dragon" motor launch shoots up Honey's canoe, she accompanies Bond and Quarrel on their trek across the island.

E. As Honey tells Bond her backstory, there are also further variations on move C as Bond kills one of Dr. No's men and the "dragon" kills Quarrel.

F. Dr. No's men capture Bond and Honey, who are taken to the villain's headquarters and put through a decontamination process to cleanse them of radioactive elements picked up in the swamp. Bond and Honey meet Dr. No, who explains that his scheme to topple American space launches from Cape Canaveral is to demonstrate the power of SPECTRE (Special Executive for Counterintelligence, Terrorism, Revenge, and Extortion).

G. Dr. No has Honey taken away ("I am sure the guards will amuse her") and imprisons Bond, who escapes from his cell by crawling through the ventilation system.

H. Bond disguises himself as one of Dr. No's men and enters the laboratory, where he deliberately overloads the power elements of the nuclear reactor. Bond fights Dr. No and kills him in the boiling nuclear fuel rod pool. Bond rescues Honey, while a chain reaction from the laboratory causes the base to explode.

I. Bond and Honey escape in a motor launch. They are found by Leiter and a Royal Navy launch, but Bond lets the tow rope slip through his fingers as he and Honey drift out to sea.

Bond's escape from his cell is much simplified from the novel: he experiences an electric shock, a surge of water, and heat burns, but it is never stated explicitly that this was an obstacle course devised by Dr. No to test his endurance. Bond and Honey escape from Crab Key in a motor launch rather than by commandeering the marsh buggy as in the novel.

The film's narrative similarity to the book probably made it inevitable that it would replicate the latter's ideological structures and patterns, with a partial realignment. In terms of social class—historically the dominant thematic preoccupation of British cinema—*Dr. No* aligns itself with the processes of social change taking place in the postwar years as Britain adjusted to the growth of mass consumption and the emergence of a society based on meritocracy rather than privilege. The early Bond films reconfigure the social politics of the novels: the Bond of the films is less deferential toward authority and less overtly patriotic than his literary counterpart (or rather, his patriotism takes on an ironic slant that is rarely evident in the books). In the process he becomes—as David Buxton argues—a classless and modernizing figure:

> By the 1950s, the amateur spy had given way to the professional technician, but what is striking about the James Bond character is the confusion over his class status. Whereas Bond appears to be something of an "aristocratic clubman" in the Fleming novels, a continuation of the tradition of "snobbery with violence," he takes on a more "man of the people" aspect in the Sean Connery film versions, a "classless" moderniser.[19]

Connery's Bond represents a form of classless masculinity that reflects the social changes of the 1960s: he sits outside the social coordinates of British society (and British cinema) insofar as he is neither a patrician officer-class type (the sort of characters played by actors such as Jack Hawkins or Richard Todd) nor a working-class rebel of the sort seen in the new wave films (exemplified by actors such as Albert Finney, Tom Courtenay, and Richard Harris). Connery's Scots heritage is also a significant factor here: his soft Edinburgh accent—which, as we have seen, confused some reviewers, who thought he was Irish or Irish-American—is neither cut-glass Home Counties nor heavily class-inflected regional English.

Connery's casting as Bond was undoubtedly serendipitous: *Dr. No* would probably still have succeeded with another actor in the star role but it might have been a different type of film. Connery embodies a style of screen heroism that was new to British cinema. As Andrew Rissik observes: "*Dr. No* effectively marked the end for the kind of arid stardom that actors like Leslie Howard had epitomised, and in which Britain had persistently traded. It declared a whole tradition obsolete, a tradition that had associated chivalry with polite vowels and a decorous repression of passion, overt sexuality and any real kind of spontaneous physical action."[20] Connery's performance detaches Bond from the sexless "good chap" masculinity exemplified by previous British screen stars such as Ronald Colman and Kenneth More in favor of the more virile appeal of Hollywood stars such as Clark Gable, Errol Flynn, and Steve McQueen. Connery acknowledged that it was Terence Young who "took me in hand and knocked me into shape with his tailor [Anthony Sinclair] and the Turnbull & Asser shirts and all the gear."[21] At the same time, Young is keen to emphasize Connery's physique:

he appears shirtless in several scenes and for most of the second half of the film is wearing cut-off cotton trousers and a tight-fitting polo shirt (figure 6.3). Connery was unique for a British actor of the period in that he was able to convey Bond's sophistication and toughness with equal conviction. Broccoli averred that this quality was the reason for his casting: "To put it in the vernacular of our profession: Sean had the balls for the part ... The whole point of having Sean in the role, with his strong physical magnetism and the overtones of a truck driver, was that it thrilled the women, but, more important, young men in the audience could feel there was a guy up there like them."[22]

A similar break with tradition can be seen in the film's representation of women. For Sue Harper, "The Bond films of the 1960s cut sexuality loose from its connections with class, which

FIGURE 6.3 *Dr. No* took every opportunity to display Sean Connery's "strong physical magnetism." *Dr. No* (Danjaq LLC/United Artists Corporation, 1962).

are so evident in other films of the period."²³ *Dr. No* establishes the different archetypes of femininity that would come to define the Bond films. Sylvia Trench (Eunice Gayson) is a secondary character created for the film, but her description in the script ("willowy, exquisitely gowned, with a classic, deceptively cold beauty") recalls Fleming characters such as Vesper Lynd (*Casino Royale*) and Gala Brand (*Moonraker*). Sylvia is worldly, sophisticated, financially independent, and unafraid to make clear her sexual interest in Bond ("Looks like you're out to get me"; "It's an idea at that"). Miss Taro (Zena Marshall) exemplifies villainous femininity, which here is associated with racial otherness, as her dialogue and the furnishings of her apartment identify her as Chinese. (Marshall was an English actress but possessed the sort of looks often described as "exotic," which led to her being cast in Asian roles.) The character allows herself to be seduced by Bond in an attempt to murder him. However, the most memorable "Bond girl" in *Dr. No*—indeed, the most memorable in all the films—is Ursula Andress as Honey Rider. As in the book, Honey is a child of nature rather than a sophisticated woman of the world. The film is less insistent than the book on presenting Honey as sexually "out of place": the incident of her rape is alluded to briefly—and her retribution ("I put a Black Widow spider underneath his mosquito net—a female and they're the worst. It took him a whole week to die")—but she does not bear the visible reminder of a broken nose. However, Honey ultimately has less agency than in the book insofar as she no longer effects her own escape from Dr. No's death-trap and has to be rescued by Bond.

However, the attempt to position women as progressive and liberated is undercut by the film's blatant sexism. *Dr. No* reinforces the tendency already noted in the novel to present women as sexualized objects. Andress represents a male fantasy of female sexuality that aligns closely with the outlook of *Playboy* magazine: well-scrubbed, large-breasted, long-haired, and non-prudish about her body. As Claire Hines observes in her study of Bond and *Playboy*: "Like the Playmates in *Playboy*, gazed at by Bond in *Dr. No*, Honey Rider looks beautiful and seductive, but also appears innocently naïve . . . [There] is no question that above all, cast as Honey Rider, Andress's physical appearance and beauty made an unforgettable first impression."[24] Her introduction, emerging from the sea wearing an ivory-white cotton bikini, has become one of the iconic moments of the Bond films. Terence Young felt that it was "the greatest woman's entrance in a picture."[25] Michael Denning's argument that the erotic content of the books focuses on Bond's role as voyeur applies equally to the film of *Dr. No*. Indeed, the privileging of Bond's point of view is inscribed in the script:

146. BOND'S EYELINE. DAY.
What he sees: HONEY, standing at the water's edge, her back to him. She is naked except for a wisp of home-made bikini with an undersea knife in a sheath . . . Her ash-blonde hair hangs to her shoulders, a little wet and bedraggled. Her skin is deep honey coloured. A diving mask is pushed up onto her forehead. At her feet lies a heap of small pink shells.[26]

The scene as shot differs slightly in the film in that Honey is facing the camera rather than standing with her back to it (figure 6.4). And, of course, the dictates of censorship mandated that she could not be entirely nude as per the book. Nevertheless, the cinematic Bond follows the literary Bond and bears a "licence to look": Bond's point of view is privileged. That the film itself is entirely complicit in this process is indicated in the ensuing dialogue between Honey ("Are you looking for shells too?") and Bond's knowing reply ("No, I'm just looking").

Laura Mulvey's influential article "Visual Pleasure and Narrative Cinema," published in 1975, is a formative text of feminist film theory. Mulvey draws upon psychoanalytical theories of scopophilia (gaining pleasure from the act of looking) to argue that mainstream film plays out a scopophilic impulse: the cinematic

FIGURE 6.4 Ursula Andress as Honey Rider: an object of "to-be-looked-at-ness." *Dr. No* (Danjaq LLC/United Artists Corporation, 1962).

apparatus is structured around an explicitly gendered form of spectatorship in which point of view is associated with a male spectator while women function as eroticized objects of desire. In this reading, cinema constructs a dominant "male gaze" and women become passive objects of "to-be-looked-at-ness":

> In a world ordered by sexual imbalance, pleasure in looking has been split between active/male and passive/female. The determining male gaze projects its fantasy onto the female figure, which is styled accordingly. In their traditional exhibitionist role women are simultaneously looked at and displayed, with their appearance coded for strong visual and erotic impact so that they can be said to connote *to-be-looked-at-ness*. Woman displayed as sexual object is the leitmotif of erotic spectacle: from pin-ups to strip-tease, from Ziegfeld to Busby Berkeley, she holds the look, plays to and signifies male desire. Mainstream film neatly combined spectacle and narrative.[27]

Dr. No seems on the face of it a textbook example of this process insofar as the male gaze is institutionalized both in the script ("BOND'S EYELINE . . . What he sees") and in the film itself ("No, I'm just looking"). It might even be argued that the Bond films would have made a better test case for Mulvey's thesis than the Josef Von Sternberg and Alfred Hitchcock films she uses as examples, which are hardly representative of classical Hollywood.[28]

Yet, on closer analysis, even a film such as *Dr. No* turns out to be more complex in terms of gendered spectatorship than it would first appear. There are several instances where Bond is the object of a woman's gaze—the female photographer at the airport taking his picture, the receptionist at the hotel in Kingston whose admiring look follows him across the lobby, the scene where Honey watches him as he washes in the river—and one where another man, Dr. No, studies Bond's sleeping body. (The film omits the villain studying Honey's body in the same way.) In this sense, the film is more inclined to present Bond's body as an object of the gaze (including both female and male) than is the book, where Honeychile is denied the opportunity of looking at Bond's body and interprets his reluctance to undress before her as fear: "I wonder why he's frightened. Of course if I wrestled with him I'd win easily . . . Perhaps he's not really very strong. His arms and chest look strong enough. I haven't seen the rest yet. Perhaps it's weak. Yes, that must be it. That's why he doesn't dare take his clothes off in front of me."[29]

It is hardly insightful to observe that the Bond films construct a traditionally structured patriarchal social order: Bond is the self-assured dominant male and women know their place. It might be that the reason why some critics regard the Bond films with such antipathy is that the series makes no attempt to disguise its sexism. However, this aspect of the films was not necessarily an aberration. Other British genre films of the 1960s—including the "Carry On" comedies and Hammer horrors—have similarly problematic sexual politics. Even the new wave films—generally seen as representing the socially progressive trend of British film culture at the time—have been found wanting in this respect. John Hill has argued that this movement's interest in working-class masculinity has the effect of privileging a male point of view and marginalizing female characters, whose treatment in the films borders on the misogynistic. Hill suggests that the women of the new wave are no less stereotyped than those in the Bond films: they tend to be either dutiful wives/girlfriends or more sexually experienced lovers/mistresses. He notes that "the women themselves can become something of a commodity, desired not so much for themselves as for the economic advantages they represent."[30] Furthermore, the resentment felt by male protagonists at being forced into marriage and consequent social conformity often takes expression in verbal or physical violence toward women. Hill contends that "there was more than a streak of misogyny running through the films and a failure to acknowledge the changing social and economic role of women in British society other than as consumers."[31] To this extent, *Dr. No* is really no worse than the new wave films: Bond treats women as disposable commodities, but he does not hate them.[32]

The picture's politics of race are even more problematic than those of gender. As in other aspects of the adaptation into film, *Dr. No* offers a partial realignment of the politics of the book. Fleming's description of the racial and social hierarchies of Jamaica is omitted, as is much of the book's casual racism. Nevertheless, the film is still framed within a colonialist worldview: it is one of only two Bond films (with *Thunderball*) set predominantly in a British colony under direct rule. The colonial locations of the book—Government House, Queen's Club—remain intact, and the film is equally inaccurate in its representation of the system of government in Jamaica. Raymond

Durgnat was the first critic to highlight the reactionary racial politics of *Dr. No* in his book *A Mirror for England*:

> Whatever Brand X critics may have written, Bond isn't just an Organization Man, but a rigid jingoist, almost loveably archaic. If you have forelocks, prepare to touch them now, in fond farewell to the Edwardiana in modern drag lovingly panoplied forth in the first half of *Dr. No* (1962) as Bond glides along the Establishment's Old Boy Net. The British Raj, reduced to its Caribbean enclave, lords it benevolently over jovial and trusting West Indians and faithful coloured police-sergeants, the Uncle Toms of Dock Green. We might almost be back with Lieutenant Kenneth More on the North-West Frontier. Meanwhile out on Crab Key lurks Dr. No, last of the war lords, whose "chigro" minions . . . blend of the Yellow Peril and the Mau-Mau, battle it out with his English co-anachronism.[33]

In fact, the film does not use the racially offensive term "Chigro" and there is no explicit reference to Dr. No's connections to the Chinese community in Jamaica. However, the *Daily Gleaner*'s review anticipated—and rejected—Durgnat's categorization of "the Uncle Toms of Dock Green" (a reference to the long-running BBC police series *Dixon of Dock Green*) when it commented that local actor William Foster-Davis, cast as Superintendent Duff, seemed "more like a Police Officer than most real life Police Officers do."[34]

James Robertson has argued that the differences between novel and film "demonstrate how the verities of the cold war and the glamour of high technology encouraged the overwriting of elements in his [Fleming's] original plot that engaged with specifically Jamaican concerns during the endgame of Britain's empire."[35] A few glimpses of the "real" Jamaica remain in the opening sequence as the camera follows the "three blind mice" from downtown Kingston to Queen's Club and in the brief inclusion of the local music scene as Byron Lee's calypso band performs for the racially diverse clientele of Pus-Feller's nightclub. Bond receives precise directions from Miss Taro ("You take the Port Royal Road out of Kingston, then the Windward Road, until you get to the cement factory, then you turn left . . ."). This is to lure the agent into an ambush on a road still under construction, but it also locates the incident in a real place, in contrast to the fictional geography of Crab Key. These elements of the film might be seen as a legacy of the documentary aspects of Fleming's books, which were always characterized by a strong sense of place. However, the Jamaican reception of *Dr. No* seems not to have been particularly concerned with the film's cultural authenticity (or lack thereof), but instead reveled in its depiction of the island as a space of exotic and colorful fantasy. Here is the *Daily Gleaner* again: "It mightn't seem much like the place you live in, but for Secret Agent 007 [Jamaica] was the most exciting spot in the 1963 film world of mass murder and revenge. My bet is it will make you feel that way too."[36]

The character who comes out of the adaptation worst is Quarrel. His role is diminished by the inclusion of Felix Leiter—a consequence of the film's geopolitical realignment toward the United States—and in the process he becomes a rum-swilling, rolling-eyed racial stereotype who is treated by Bond as little more than a lackey, with none of the mutual respect and affection evident in the novel. At one point, Bond even orders Quarrel: "Fetch my shoes!" Quarrel is characterized as superstitious (it is he rather than Honey who first mentions Dr. No's feared dragon) and he takes Dutch courage from a keg of rum. John Kitzmiller's performance approximates Quarrel's speech patterns described by Fleming in the book ("I gets my directions from my nose, my hears, my hinstincts"), but the script allows him little opportunity to develop the character (figure 6.5). The undermining of the book's most sympathetic and strongest Black character is the most regrettable aspect

FIGURE 6.5 Bond and Quarrel (John Kitzmiller). The Cayman Islander's role is diminished from the novel. *Dr. No* (Danjaq LLC/United Artists Corporation, 1962).

of *Dr. No*, especially at a time when British films such as *Sapphire* (1959) had started to offer more progressive representations of race.

The contest between Bond and the villain, one of the ideological structures identified by Umberto Eco in the books, is also overlaid with a racialized dimension. Joseph Wiseman's Dr. No is less grotesque than the figure in the novel. The specter of the "Yellow Peril" is less emphasized, though Wiseman does wear "oriental" eye makeup. Nevertheless, he still clearly represents an association between villainy and ethnic otherness: his Nehru jacket with high Mandarin collar—a fashion associated with Indian Prime Minister Jawaharlal Nehru—would become the garment of choice for other fashion-conscious Bond villains, including Kamal Khan (*Octopussy*, 1983) and Elliot Carver (*Tomorrow Never Dies*, 1997), as well as Dr. Evil in the Austin Powers spoofs (figure 6.6).[37] Bond's meeting with Dr. No also presents an opportunity for Bondian snobbery when he is admonished for picking up a champagne bottle as a weapon:

DR. NO
That's a Dom Perignon '55, it would be a pity to break it.

BOND
I prefer the '53 myself.

This is more than just an example of the winesmanship that would become a recurring feature of the films. (In *From Russia with Love*, for example, Bond realizes that Grant is a villain when he orders red Chianti with Dover sole.) Bond's assertion

FIGURE 6.6 Joseph Wiseman as Dr. No. The Nehru jacket associates the character with a tradition of oriental villainy. *Dr. No* (Danjaq LLC/United Artists Corporation, 1962).

of his superior taste is a rejoinder to the foreign Dr. No that Western values will inevitably triumph in the end.

Dr. No might therefore seem to be a particularly insidious example of a common enough phenomenon in popular cinema: a film where the pleasures offered by a sumptuous visual style and decorative mise-en-scène are in marked contrast to the conservative, even reactionary politics underpinning the narrative. For some academic commentators, indeed, *Dr. No*'s politics are so egregious that they have difficulty in reconciling this with the film's popularity: "And yet, apparently, Bond fans routinely derive enormous pleasure as they negotiate the strange spectatorial sublime that is James Bond's complicated cinematic treatment of race and otherness, white male privilege and toxic masculinity, Anglo-American racial superiority and cool Britishness."[38] Yet, much the same sort of observation could be made of most popular genres: the misogyny often inherent in the horror film and the racist ideology that underpins the Western have not prevented those genres from being claimed as sites of significant cultural interest. And the racial politics of some box-office blockbusters, including action-adventure movies such as *Raiders of the Lost Ark* (1981) and *True Lies* (1994), are no less problematic than those of *Dr. No*. Even the Blaxploitation cycle of the 1970s that placed African-American characters at the center of the narrative has been accused of perpetuating negative racial stereotypes. In other words, the Bond films are not uniquely problematic texts when it comes to squaring the politics of films with their popular appeal.

It would be naïve to assume that the cinemagoers who made *Dr. No* such a popular success in the early 1960s were all blind to the film's racism. In this context, it needs to be borne in mind that it was popular not just in a Britain coming to terms with its postimperial identity, but also in the United States at the time of the emergence of the civil rights movement and (according to the local press) in Jamaica in the immediate aftermath of independence. What this popularity does highlight, perhaps, are the different interests and concerns of academic film studies and "real" audiences. For, while academic critics in the twenty-first century have read *Dr. No* largely through the lens of postcolonial studies and critical race theory, from which perspective its ideological shortcomings are all too apparent, audiences of the 1960s seem to have responded positively to the film's visual invention, its unashamed permissiveness, its radical departure from the realist orthodoxy of British cinema, and its projection of a classless modernity that situated it within a moment of profound and far-reaching change not only in British cinema but also in society at large.

CONCLUSION

THIS BOOK has argued that *Dr. No* deserves to be seen in its historical and cultural contexts, and that its success was no happy accident, but rather was the outcome of a deliberate and carefully planned strategy to turn Ian Fleming's novel into a highly commercial screen entertainment. In the process, it has debunked some of the myths and misconceptions around the film's production. In particular, it has challenged the narrative—promoted by the Bond producers themselves—that the film industry did not recognize the commercial potential of *Dr. No*. This may be because Harry Saltzman and Cubby Broccoli wanted to present an image of themselves as visionary producers and risk-takers in contrast to a film industry that was both economically cautious and culturally conservative. Or it may simply reflect how the film industry attempts to create its own mythology: the narrative that a successful formula is discovered through some form of alchemy is a seductive one that disguises the industrial and ideological processes at work in the production of any particular film. In any event, the idea that the success of *Dr. No* took the industry by surprise does not bear close scrutiny.

Dr. No is the sort of film that disproves the auteur theory: the idea that the director is the prime creative influence on the making of a film. Its production history demonstrates the nature of filmmaking as a collective and collaborative exercise. Its style certainly owed much to Terence Young's direction, but it also depended upon the production design of Ken Adam, the cinematography of Ted Moore, the editing of Peter Hunt, and the musical contributions of Monty Norman and John Barry. Four writers (five if we include Fleming as author of the source text) also contributed in varying degrees to the finished film. The fact that the Bond films do not lend themselves easily to a traditional auteurist reading may be one reason why they were for so long marginalized in academic film studies. For Andrew Sarris, the leading American champion of the auteur theory, Terence Young was little more than a commercial hack who "did the best of the Bonds, *Wait Until Dark*, and the curiously memorable, baroque, and unoriginal *Corridor of Mirrors*. He seems at home with the sweet lyricism of death, but his overall career is staggeringly undistinguished. Nevertheless, he seems to have come into his own, at least commercially."[1]

Looking back at *Dr. No* on the occasion of its sixtieth anniversary, what is perhaps most remarkable is how fresh the film still seems today. It may be less polished than the films that followed, its racial politics are undeniably problematic, and Sean Connery is still not quite the finished article as Bond (his performances in *From Russia with Love* and *Goldfinger* are more

CONCLUSION

confident and relaxed). But it is economical in its storytelling, it establishes the archetypes of the Bond villain and the Bond girl, and it is a tour de force of production design. The historical significance of *Dr. No* is twofold. It demonstrated—alongside other films of the time such as *The Guns of Navarone* and *Zulu*—that the combination of American finance and British talent could produce films that would succeed in the international market. And it effectively gave birth to a new genre: the contemporary high-tech action-adventure thriller. In this sense, *Dr. No* was not only the prototype of the Bond series, but also of what screenwriter Larry Gross called "the Big Loud Action Movie": it marked the beginning of "an entirely new superkinetic cartoon-type action movie" that is now one of the staple genres of the film industry.[2]

The transformative effect that *Dr. No* had on popular cinema is perhaps best expressed by its director Terence Young in one of the last interviews before his death in 1994. And this seems an appropriate point on which to conclude:

> I got a phone call from Orson [Welles] . . . And before we'd even started dinner, Orson Welles said straight out: "I want to tell you something." He said: "I've seen your picture and in a strange way it's changed the vocabulary of cinema." I didn't quite really know what he meant until much later on. But he said something very shrewd afterwards. Orson was a very good film critic, by the way, he would have made a marvellous critic. He said: "You'll find within two years every film of this type will try to imitate this style, and in the end they'll do it better than you." He was probably right.[3]

Appendix I

DR. NO PRODUCTION CREDITS

Production company: Eon Productions
Distributor: United Artists
Producers: Harry Saltzman and Albert R. Broccoli
Director: Terence Young
Screenplay: Richard Maibaum, Johanna Harwood, Berkely Mather
Based on the novel by: Ian Fleming
Director of photography: Ted Moore, BSC
Production design: Ken Adam
Production manager: L. C. Rudkin
Editor: Peter Hunt
Main title designed by: Maurice Binder
Animation: Trevor Bond
Assistant director: Clive Reed
Camera operator: John Winbolt
Continuity: Helen Whitson

DR. NO PRODUCTION CREDITS

Make-up: John O'Gorman
Hair stylist: Eileen Warwick
Sound recordists: Wally Milner, John Dennis
Costume: Tessa Welborn
Set dressing: Freda Pearson
Dubbing editors: Archie Ludski, Norman Wanstall
Assistant editor: Ben Reyner
Special effects: Frank George
Music composed by: Monty Norman
Conducted by: Eric Rodgers
Orchestrated by: Brent Rhodes
"James Bond Theme" played by John Barry & Orchestra

CREDITED CAST

Sean Connery (James Bond)
Ursula Andress (Honey Rider)
Joseph Wiseman (Dr. No)
Jack Lord (Felix Leiter)
Bernard Lee (M)
Anthony Dawson (Professor Dent)
Zena Marshall (Miss Taro)
John Kitzmiller (Quarrel)
Eunice Gayson (Sylvia Trench)
Lois Maxwell (Miss Moneypenny)
Peter Burton (Major Boothroyd)
Yvonne Shima (Sister Lily)
Michel Mok (Sister Rose)

DR. NO PRODUCTION CREDITS

Marguerite Le Wars (Photographer)
William Foster-Davis (Superintendent Duff)
Dolores Keator (Mary)
Reginald Carter (Jones)
Louis Blaazer (Pleydell-Smith)
Colonel Burton (General Potter)

UNCREDITED CAST

Timothy Moxon (Strangways)
Eric Coverley (1st Beggar)
Charles Edghill (2nd Beggar)
Henry Lopez (3rd Beggar)
Adrian Robinson (Hearse Driver)
Maxwell Shaw (Foreman of Signals)
John Hatton (Radio Operator)
Simon Martin (Messenger, Les Ambassadeurs)
Stanley Morgan (Attendant, Les Ambassadeurs)
Lester Prendergast (Pus-Feller)
Malou Pantera (Hotel Receptionist)
Frank Singuineau (Hotel Waiter)
Bettine Le Beau (Dent's Receptionist)
Carol Reckard (Dent's Boatman)
Lancelot Evans (Jetty Guard)
Carey Robinson (1st Patrol Boatman)
Levi Murray (Machine-Gunner)
Keith Binns (1st Dog Handler)
Abbot Anderson (2nd Dog Handler)

DR. NO PRODUCTION CREDITS

Lachlan McNeil (3rd Dog Handler)
K. E. S. Chin (1st Dragon Driver)
Louis Marriott (2nd Dragon Driver)
Arnold Lee (1st Decontamination Operative)
Anthea Blandice (2nd Decontamination Operative)
Milton Reid (Dr. No's Bodyguard)
Donald Chin (Chang)
Anthony Chinn (Main Controller)

Appendix II

DR. NO PRODUCTION BUDGET

THE "FINAL PRODUCTION BUDGET" for *Dr. No* as submitted by Eon Productions to Film Finances on December 12, 1961, was broken down as follows:

A. Story and Script	£49,365
B. Producer and Director Fees	£31,786
C. Production Unit Salaries	
1. Production Management and Secretaries	£4,024
2. Assistant Directors and Continuity	£1,865
3. Technical Advisers	£397
4. Camera Crews	£3,281
5. Recording Crews	£3,602
6. Editing Staff	£3,878
7. Still Camera Staff	£707
8. Wardrobe Designer and Staff	£1,400
9. Make-up Artists	£779

DR. NO PRODUCTION BUDGET

  10. Hairdressers   £449
  11. Casting   £625
  12. Production Accountancy   £3,430
  13. Projectionists   £325
  14. Other Staff   £250
  15. Foreign Unit Technicians   £1,568
D. Set Dressing and Supervisory Staff Salaries   £5,877
E. Artistes
  1. Cast   £25,000
  2. Stand-ins and Doubles   £664
  3. Crowd   £1,200
F. Orchestra and Composer   £1,190
G. Costumes and Wigs   £1,250
H. Miscellaneous Production Stores   £1,365
I. Film and Laboratory Charges   £14,656
J. Studio Rentals   £16,750
K. Equipment   £4,738
L. Power   £750
M. Travel and Transport   £20,182
N. Hotel and Living Expenses   £47,614
O. Insurances   £8,710
P. Holiday and Sick Pay   £1,350
Q. Publicity Salaries and Expenses   £1,156
R. Miscellaneous Expenses   £4,100
S. Sets and Models
  1. Labour – Construction   £8,000
  2. Labour – Dressing   £1,000
  3. Labour – Operating   £3,100
  4. Labour – Striking   £500

DR. NO PRODUCTION BUDGET

5. Labour – Lighting	£2,995
6. Labour – Lamp Spotting	[*left blank in original*]
7. Foreign Unit Labour	£1,200
8. Materials – Construction	£4,500
9. Properties	£4,500
T. Special Location Facilities	£1,100
TOTAL DIRECT COST:	£273,906
Y. Finance and Legal Charges	£16,255
Z. Overheads	£5,000
Production Contingency Allowance	£22,198
TOTAL	£317,359

■ ■ ■

Although labelled "Final Production Budget," the amount was subsequently adjusted upward to £321,277 following consultation with Film Finances. A further increase brought the actual final budget to £322,069.

Appendix III

DR. NO DAILY PROGRESS REPORTS

THE FILM FINANCES ARCHIVE holds a nearly complete set of the daily progress reports for *Dr. No* filed by production manager L. C. Rudkin. These reports document the day-to-day shooting of the film on location and in the studio. The location reports for February 5 and 6 are missing, though the call sheets indicate the scenes and the names of the actors on set.

KEY

AA (Abbot Anderson), AB (Anthea Blandice), AC (Anthony Chin), AD (Anthony Dawson), AL (Arnold Lee), AR (Adrian Robinson), BL (Bernard Lee), BS (Bob Simmons), CB (Colonel Burton), CE (Charles Edghill), CR (Carol Reckard), CRo (Carey Robinson), DC (Donald Chin), DK (Dolores Keator), EC (Eric Caverley), EL (Easton Lee), FS (Frank Singuineau),

HL (Harry Locke), HLo (Henry Lopez), JH (John Hatton), JK (John Kitzmiller), JL (Jack Lord), JN (Juliet Nixon), JW (Joseph Wiseman), KB (Keith Binns), KC (K. E. S. Chin), LB (Louis Blaazer), LE (Lancelot Evans), LM (Louis Marriott), LMa (Lois Maxwell), LMc (Lachlan McNeil), LMu (Levi Murray), LP (Lester Prendergast), MLW (Marguerite Le Wars), MM (Michele Mok), MP (Malou Pantera), MR (Milton Reid), MS (Maxwell Shaw), MVDZ (Monica Van Der Zyl), PB (Peter Burton), RC (Reggie Carter), RR (Robert Rietti), SC (Sean Connery), SM (Simon Martin), SMo (Stanley Morgan), TM (Timothy Moxon), UA (Ursula Andress), WFD (William Foster-Davies), YS (Yvonne Shima), ZM (Zena Marshall).

LOCATION

Tues 16.01.1962: Kingston airport (SC, JL, JK, MLW, RC).

Weds 17.01.1962: Airport—roads and side road (SC, JL, JK, RC. MLW, BS).

Thurs 18.01.1962: Airport—road and side road (SC, RC, BS).

Fri 19.01.1962: Ext. Quarrel's harbour (SC, JL, JK).

Sat 20.01.1962: Ext. open sea (SC, JL, JK).

Mon 22.01.1962: Ext. open sea (SC, JL, JK). Ext. Strangways house (WFD, EC, EL, HL).

Tues 23.01.1962: Int/ext. Pus-Feller's (Morgan's Harbour) (SC, JL, JK, MLW, LP).

DR. NO DAILY PROGRESS REPORTS

Weds 24.01.1962: Int/ext. Pus-Feller's (SC, JL, JK, MLW, LP).

Thurs 25.01.1962: Int/ext. Pus-Feller's (SC, JL, JK).

Fri 26.01.1962: Ext. airport road (SC, JL, JK). Ext. King's House (SC, RC).

Sat 27.01.1962: Ext. coast road (SC, EC, AR).

Mon 29.01.1962: Int. Queen's Club (SC, TM, LB, AD, CB).

Tues 30.01.1962: Ext. Queen's Club. Ext. Kingston streets (SC, JL, JK, ML, LP, TM, EC, CE, HL, AR).

Weds 31.01.1962: Ext: coast road (SC, EC, CE). Ext. Courtleigh Manor (Bond's hotel).

Thurs 01.02.1962: Ext. Kingston streets. Ext. airport road. Ext. Bond's hotel (SC, EC, CE, HL).

Fri 02.02.1962: Ext. open sea (end sequence) (SC, JL, JK, UA).

Sat 03.02.1962: Ext. open sea (end sequence). Ext. airport road. Ext. Strangways' house (5 Kinsala Avenue) (SC, JL, UA, RC, EC, CE, HLo, WFD).

Sun 04.02.1962: Int. Strangways' house (SC, EC, CE, HLo, WFD, DK).

Mon 05.02.1962: Ext. Strangways. Int. Pus-Feller's (SC, JK, WFD, EC, CE, HLo).

Tues 06.02.1962: Int. Pus-Feller's (SC, JL, JK, LP)

Weds 07.02.1962: Ext. Dent's harbour (AD, CR) Ext. open sea (SC, JL, UA).

Thurs 08.02.1962: Ext. beach—Crab Key (Laughing Waters) (SC, UA, JK).

Fri 09.02.1962: Ext. beach—Crab Key (Laughing Waters) (SC, UA, JK).

Sat 10.02.1962: Ext. beach—Crab Key (Laughing Waters) (SC, UA, JK, CRo).

Mon 12.02.1962: Ext. beach—Crab Key (Laughing Waters) (SC, UA, JK).

Tues 13.02.1962: Ext. mangrove swamp (SC, UA, JK, KC, LM).

Weds 14.02.1962: Ext. mangrove swamp (SC, UA, JK, KC, LM).

Thurs 15.02.1962: Ext. mangrove swamp (SC, UA, JK, KC, LM).

Fri 16.02.1962: Ext. jungle river (White River) (SC, UA, JK, KB, AA).

Sat 17.02.1962: Ext. Ext. jungle river (White River) (SC, UA, JK, KB, AA, LMc).

Sun 18.02.1962: Ext. Crab Key dock (SC, UA, AD, CR, LE).

Mon 19.02.1962: Ext. Coral Beach and headland. Ext. Bauxite dock (SC, UA, JK, CR, AD, LE, LMu).

Tues 20.02.1962: Ext. waterfall hide-out and river (SC, UA, JK).

Weds 21.02.1962: Ext. Miss Taro's. Ext. beach—Crab Key (SC, UA, JK, AD).

Unit left Kingston on Friday, February 23, 1962 on a Britannia charter flight at 5:20 p.m. and arrived at the London airport on Saturday, February 24 at 2:15 p.m.

STUDIO

Mon 26.02.1962: Pinewood Stage D. Int. M's Office (SC, BL, PB).

Tues 27.02.1962: Stage D. Int. M's Office (SC, BL, PB, LM).

Weds 28.02.1962: Stage D. Int. Dent's Office (SC, AD). Int. Communications Room (MS, JH).

Thurs 01.03.1962: Stage D. Int. Communications Room (MS, JH). Int. Bond's Flat (SC, EG).

Fri 02.03.1962: Stage D. Int: Les Ambassadeurs (SC, EG, SM, SMo).

Mon 05.03.1962: Stage D. Les Ambassadeurs (SC, EG).

Tues 06.03.1962: Stage A. Int. Miss Taro's House (SC, ZM)

Weds 07.03.1962: Stage A. Int. Miss Taro's (SC, ZM, AD).

Thurs 08.03.1962: Stage A. Int. Miss Taro's (SC, ZM, AD).

Fri 09.03.1962: Stages A and D. Int. Reception Centre (SC, UA, MM, YS, AB).

Mon 12.03.1962: Stage A. Int. Dr. No's apartment. Int Dr. No's reception (SC, JW, AD).

Tues 13.03.1962: Stage A. Int. Dr. No's apartment (SC, UA, JW, MR).

Weds 14.02.1962: Stage A. Int. Dr. No's apartment (SC, UA, JW, MR, DC).

Thurs 15.02.1962: Stages A and C. Int. Dr. No's apartment. Int. Decontamination Centre (SC, UA, JW, MR, DC, AB, AC, AL).

Fri 16.02.1962: Stage C. Int. Decontamination Centre (SC, UA, DC, AB, AC, AL)

Mon 19.03.1962: Stage D. Int, Guest Suite (SC, UA, YS).

Tues 20.03.1962: Stage D. Int. Guest Suite. Int. Bond's hotel room (SC, JW, FS).

Weds 21.03.1962: Stage E. Int. Reactor Room (SC, JW, DC, AC).

Thurs 22.03.1962: Stage E. Int. Reactor Room (SC, JW, DC, AC).

Fri 23.03.1962: Stage E. Int. Reactor Room (SC, JW, DC, AC).

Mon 26.03.196:. Stages E and D. Int. Reactor Room. Ints lift, airlock. Int. Pleydell-Smith's office (SC, UA, JW, LB, WFD).

Tues 27.03.1962: Stage D. Int. Pleydell-Smith's office (SC, ZM, LB, WFD).

Weds 28.03.1962: Stage D. Int. Bond's hotel foyer. Int. cell (SC, UA, MP).

Thurs 29.03.1962: Stage D. Int. cell and shaft. Ext. jungle river (SC, UA).

Fri 30.03.1962: Stage D. Int. shaft. Int. Crab Room (SC, UA, AB).

Mon 02.04.1962: Stage D. Int. Crab Room (SC, UA, AB).

Tues 03.04.1962: Stage D. Int. Bond's hotel room. Ext—boat (SC, UA).

Thurs 05.04.1962: Stills (SC, UA). Post-synch (UA).

Fri 06.04.1962: Post-synch (UA).

DR. NO DAILY PROGRESS REPORTS

Mon 16.04.1962: Post-synch (MVDZ)
Tues 17.04.1962: Post-synch (MVDZ)

Tues 24.04.1962: Post-synch (MS, JN, RR, FS)
Weds 25.04.1962: Post-synch (JK, HL)
Thurs 26.04.1962: Pick-ups and inserts (SC, AC, BS).

NOTES

INTRODUCTION

1. "James Bond's 25th Anniversary," *Hollywood Reporter*, July 14, 1987, S-26.
2. "007 Pix Rentals Hit $100,000," *Variety*, October 12, 1966, 1.
3. *30 Years of James Bond*, London Weekend Television for ITV, prod. Lorna Dickinson, October 3, 1992.
4. "Three British Films Head the General Releases," *Kine Weekly*, December 13, 1962, 7.
5. Alexander Walker, *Hollywood, England: The British Film Industry in the Sixties* (London: Michael Joseph, 1974), 189.
6. Roy Armes, *A Critical History of the British Cinema* (London: Secker & Warburg, 1978), 254.
7. "Harry Saltzman Recalls Early Coolness to Bond Features," *Variety*, May 11, 1987, 80.
8. Albert R. Broccoli, with Donald Zec, *When the Snow Melts: The Autobiography of Cubby Broccoli* (London: Boxtree, 1998), 177.
9. Richard Schenckman, "The Terence Young Interview," *Bondage* 10 (1981), 3.
10. Kristin Thompson and David Bordwell, *Film History: An Introduction* (New York: McGraw-Hill, 1994), 394.
11. "British Films Again ahead on General Release," *Kine Weekly*, December 19, 1963, 5.

INTRODUCTION

12. *Cinema Retro: Dr. No—Movie Classics Special 4*, ed. Lee Pfeiffer and Dave Worrall (2012).
13. The Noël Coward anecdote features in Steven Jay Rubin, *The James Bond Films: A Behind the Scenes History* (London: Talisman Books, 1981), 20; Lee Pfeiffer and Dave Worrall, *The Essential Bond: The Authorized Guide to the World of 007* (London: Boxtree, 1998), 16; Broccoli and Zec, *When the Snow Melts*, 161; Sinclair McKay, *The Man with the Golden Touch: How the Bond Films Conquered the World* (New York: Overlook Press, 2010), 28; Matthew Field and Ajay Chowdhury, *Some Kind of Hero: The Remarkable Story of the James Bond Films* (Stroud: The History Press, 2015), 65; and Paul Duncan, ed., *The James Bond 007 Archives* (Cologne: Taschen, 2015), 34. Only the last two provide a reference: Field and Chowdhury's source is Rubin's book, while Duncan's is Broccoli's memoir. There would therefore seem to be no authoritative original source for this oft-repeated anecdote.
14. The biographical entry for Coward in the ever-unreliable online encyclopedia Wikipedia (https://en.wikipedia.org/wiki/Noël Coward, accessed August 30, 2021) includes a slightly different version of Coward's alleged reply ("No, no, no, a thousand times no") and cites as the source *The Letters of Noël Coward* (London: Bloomsbury, 2007). However, the *Letters* do not include the apocryphal telegram: the page reference cited in the Wikipedia entry (page 310) mentions that Coward turned down the role of Colonel Nicholson in *The Bridge on the River Kwai* but makes no mention of Dr. No. The anecdote appears as an unsourced editorial comment in Noel Coward, *The Noel Coward Diaries*, ed. Graham Payn and Sheridan Morley (New York: Da Capo Press, 2000), 532. I am grateful to Katherine Harper for drawing this reference to my attention.
15. Aljean Harmetz comprehensively debunks the myths around the production of *Casablanca* in her book *Round Up the Usual Suspects: The Making of Casablanca—Bogart, Bergman, and World War II* (London: Weidenfeld & Nicolson, 1993).
16. Sheldon Hall, *Zulu: With Some Guts Behind It: The Making of the Epic Movie* (Sheffield, UK: Tomahawk Press, 2005), 377.

1. SEX, SNOBBERY, AND SADISM

1. Ian Fleming, "How to Write a Thriller," *Books and Bookmen*, May 1963, 18.
2. Tony Bennett and Janet Woollacott, *Bond and Beyond: The Political Career of a Popular Hero* (London: Macmillan, 1987), 26.

1. SEX, SNOBBERY, AND SADISM

3. John A. Sutherland, *Fiction and the Fiction Industry* (London: Athlone Press, 1978), 176.
4. "An Extremely Engaging Affair," *Times Literary Supplement*, April 17, 1953, 249.
5. "New Novels," *The Listener*, April 23, 1953, 695.
6. "Crime, Thrills and Detection," *Daily Telegraph*, May 7, 1954, 8.
7. "Crime, Thrills and Detection," *Daily Telegraph*, April 26, 1955, 10.
8. "Bonded Goods," *The Sunday Times*, March 25, 1956, 7.
9. "The End of the Affair," *Times Literary Supplement*, April 12, 1957, 230.
10. "Sapper" was the pen name of H. C. (Herman Cyril) McNeile, a Royal Engineers officer during the First World War. (Army engineers were popularly known as "Sappers.") McNeile featured his gentleman adventurer Captain Hugh "Bulldog" Drummond in a series of sensational thrillers in the 1920s and 1930s: *Bulldog Drummond, The Black Gang, The Third Round, The Final Count, The Female of the Species, Temple Tower, The Return of Bulldog Drummond, Knock-Out*, and *Bulldog Drummond at Bay*. The books and their film adaptations were very popular in their day but have since become unfashionable on account of their outdated social values. See Richard Usborne, *Clubland Heroes: A Nostalgic Study of Some Recurrent Characters in the Romantic Fiction of Dornford Yates, John Buchan and Sapper* (London: Barrie and Jenkins, 1974), 133–70. A more critical analysis can be found in Hans Bertens, "A Society of Murderers Run on Sound Conservative Lines: The Life and Times of Sapper's Bulldog Drummond," in *Twentieth-Century Suspense: The Thriller Comes of Age*, ed. Clive Bloom (London: Macmillan, 1990), 51–68.
11. Ian Fleming, *Goldfinger* (London: Penguin Classics, 2004 [1959]), 3.
12. Ian Fleming, *Moonraker* (London: Penguin Classics, 2004 [1955]), 34.
13. Ian Fleming, *Casino Royale* (London: Penguin Classics, 2004 [1953]), 159–60.
14. David Cannadine, "James Bond and the Decline of England," *Encounter* 53, no. 3 (1979): 46.
15. See Vivian Halloran, "Tropical Bond," in *Ian Fleming & James Bond: The Cultural Politics of 007*, ed. Edward P. Commantale, Stephen Watt, and Skip Williams (Bloomington: Indiana University Press, 2005), 158–77.
16. Umberto Eco, "The Narrative Structure in Fleming," in *The Bond Affair*, ed. Oreste Del Buono and Umberto Eco, trans. R. A. Downie (London: Macdonald, 1966), 37.
17. Quoted in John Pearson, *The Life of Ian Fleming* (London: Jonathan Cape, 1965), 284.

18. Andrew Lycett, *Ian Fleming* (London: Weidenfeld and Nicolson, 1995), 297.
19. "Sax Rohmer" was the pen name of Arthur Henry Ward, who wrote thirteen Fu Manchu books, from *The Mysterious Dr. Fu-Manchu* (1913) to *Emperor Fu-Manchu* (1959). Fu Manchu is another once-popular but now culturally problematic character, as the books represent a particularly racist worldview.
20. Geoffrey Boothroyd to Ian Fleming, May 23, 1956, in *The Man with the Golden Typewriter: Ian Fleming's James Bond Letters*, ed. Fergus Fleming (London: Bloomsbury, 2015), 141.
21. Ian Fleming, *Dr. No* (London: Penguin Classics, 2004 [1958]), 18.
22. "Old Tricks," *Times Literary Supplement*, April 11, 1958, 193.
23. "The Resilience of Cmdr. Bond," *Daily Telegraph*, April 11, 1958, 15.
24. "The Terrible Dr. No," *The Sunday Times*, March 30, 1958, 6.
25. "The Case of Mr. Fleming," *The Twentieth Century*, March 1958, 220–28.
26. "Sex, Snobbery and Sadism," *New Statesman*, April 4, 1958, 431–32.
27. "'The Exclusive Bond': Mr. Fleming on His Hero," *Manchester Guardian*, April 5, 1958, 6.
28. Kenneth O. Morgan, *The People's Peace: British History 1945–1990* (Oxford: Oxford University Press, 1992), 118–19.
29. Kingsley Amis, *The James Bond Dossier* (London: Jonathan Cape, 1965), 55.
30. Christopher Booker, *The Neophiliacs: A Study of the Revolution in English Life in the Fifties and Sixties* (London: Collins, 1969), 42–43.
31. Fleming, "How to Write a Thriller," 14.
32. Fleming, *Dr. No*, 79.
33. Michael Denning, *Cover Stories: Narrative and Ideology in the British Spy Thriller* (London: Routledge and Kegan Paul, 1987), 110.
34. Fleming, *Dr. No*, 105.
35. Fleming, *Dr. No*, 81, 144.
36. Fleming, *Dr. No*, 120, 233.
37. Fleming, *Dr. No*, 151.
38. Amis, *James Bond Dossier*, 102.
39. "'The Exclusive Bond,'" 4.
40. Fleming, *Dr. No*, 180.
41. Fleming, *Dr. No*, 14, 13.
42. "New Fiction," *The Times*, April 3, 1958, 13. "Room 101" refers to the site of each victim's "worst thing in the world" in the torture scenes of George Orwell's novel *1984*.

2. EVERYTHING OR NOTHING

43. Amis, *James Bond Dossier*, 23.
44. Alex Adams, "'The Sweet Tang of Rape': Torture, Survival and Masculinity in Ian Fleming's Bond Novels," *Feminist Theory* 18, no. 2 (2017): 144.
45. Amis, *James Bond Dossier*, 151.
46. Fleming, *Dr. No*, 9, 44.
47. Fleming, *Dr. No*, 180.
48. John G. Cawelti, *Adventure, Mystery and Romance: Formula Stories as Art and Popular Culture* (Chicago: University of Chicago Press, 1976), 31.
49. William Plomer to Ian Fleming, June 18, 1957, in *Man with the Golden Typewriter*, 75.
50. Fleming, *Dr. No*, 58.
51. Fleming, *Dr. No*, 34.
52. Ian Fleming, *Live and Let Die* (London: Penguin Classics, 2004 [1954]), 169.
53. Fleming, *Dr. No*, 225.
54. Fleming, *Dr. No*, 224.
55. Fleming, *Dr. No*, 57–8.
56. Census of Jamaica, April 7, 1960 (Jamaica: Department of Statistics, 1963). See also G. E. Cumper, "Preliminary Analysis of Population Growth and Social Characteristics in Jamaica, 1943–66," *Social and Economic Studies* 12, no. 4 (1963): 393–31.
57. Fleming, *Dr. No*, 2.
58. Fleming, *Dr. No*, 50, 223
59. Ian Fleming, *The Man with the Golden Gun* (London: Penguin Classics, 2006 [1965]). 40.
60. Ian Fleming to Wren Howard, May 14, 1957, in *Man with the Golden Typewriter*, 133.

2. EVERYTHING OR NOTHING

1. The "Everything or Nothing" acronym is stated as fact in Steven Jay Rubin, *The James Bond Movie Encyclopedia* (Chicago: Contemporary Books, rev. ed. 2003), 126. See also the Cubby Broccoli–endorsed Lee Pfeiffer and Philip Lisa, *The Incredible World of 007* (London: Boxtree, 1992), 14. Its persistence may be due in some measure to the "official" documentary *Everything or Nothing: The Untold Story of 007* (Red Box Films, 2012, dir. Steven Riley), produced to mark the fiftieth anniversary of the Bond series.
2. Tino Balio, *United Artists*, Volume 2: *1951–1978: The Company That Changed the Film Industry* (Madison: University of Wisconsin Press, 1987), 253–70.

2. EVERYTHING OR NOTHING

3. The Film Finances Archive, London, holds budget and cost information for several of Warwick's films, including *The Red Beret* (Realised Film Box 49), *Hell Below Zero* (Realised Film Box 66), *The Black Knight* (Realised Film Box 87), *A Prize of Gold* (Realised Film Box 118), *Safari* (Realised Film Box 151), and *The Trials of Oscar Wilde* (Realised Film Box 294). The sterling/dollar exchange rate at the time was £1 = $2.80.
4. Margaret Dickinson and Sarah Street, *Cinema and State: The Film Industry and the British Government, 1927–84* (London: British Film Institute, 1985), 225–26.
5. "Future Prospects of British Pic Prod. Remains Wrapped up in Eady Bonus," *Variety*, January 7, 1953, 191.
6. "It's Independents' Day," *Kinematograph Weekly*, December 15, 1955, 79.
7. "On Release," *Kinematograph Weekly*, February 9, 1956, 7.
8. *Boxoffice*, January 2, 1954, 1546.
9. "1954 Boxoffice Champs," *Variety*, January 5, 1955, 59; "109 Top Money Films of 1956," *Variety*, January 2, 1957, 4.
10. "Richard Maibaum: A Pretense of Seriousness," in *Backstory: Interviews with Screenwriters of Hollywood's Golden Age*, ed. Pat McGilligan (Berkeley: University of California Press, 1986), 284.
11. Albert R. Broccoli, with Donald Zec, *When the Snow Melts: The Autobiography of Cubby Broccoli* (London: Boxtree, 1998), 128.
12. "Warwick Break with Columbia," *Kinematograph Weekly*, April 18, 1957, 3; "Retrenchment by Warwick," *Kinematograph Weekly*, 24 October 1957, 3.
13. Broccoli, *When the Snow Melts*, 144–45.
14. John Osborne, *Looking Back: Never Explain, Never Apologise* (London: Faber and Faber, 1999), 151–52.
15. Tony Richardson, *Long-Distance Runner: A Memoir* (London: Faber and Faber, 1993), 96.
16. Anthony Aldgate, *Censorship and the Permissive Society: British Cinema and Theatre, 1955–1965* (Oxford: Clarendon Press, 1995), 42.
17. Quoted in Alexander Walker, *Hollywood, England: The British Film Industry in the Sixties* (London: Michael Joseph, 1974), 58.
18. Bryanston Films, revenue statement to October 31, 1965, Film Finances Archive, Realised Film Box 278: *The Entertainer*.
19. Bryanston Films, revenue statement to November 30, 1964, Film Finances Archive, Realised Film Box 289: *Saturday Night and Sunday Morning*.
20. Harry Saltzman to Bryanston Films, April 17, 1962, Film Finances Archive, Realised Film Box 289: *Saturday Night and Sunday Morning*.

2. EVERYTHING OR NOTHING

21. Quoted in "The Gilt-Edged Bond," *The Observer*, January 18, 1972, 11.
22. Andrew Lycett, *Ian Fleming* (London: Weidenfeld & Nicolson, 1995), 387.
23. Tony Bennett and Janet Woollacott, *Bond and Beyond: The Political Career of a Popular Hero* (London: Macmillan, 1987), 26.
24. Lycett, *Ian Fleming*, 382.
25. Agreement between Edward Dryhurst Productions and Harry Saltzman, June 19, 1961, Film Finances Archive, Realised Film Box 289: *Saturday Night and Sunday Morning*.
26. Robert Garrett to Peter Hope, July 4, 1961, Film Finances Archive, Realised Film Box 328: *Dr No*.
27. Saltzman to Bryanston Films, April 17, 1962.
28. Walker, *Hollywood, England*, 185.
29. Broccoli, *When the Snow Melts*, 150–51.
30. Balio, *United Artists*, 257.
31. "Broccoli-Saltzman Set Several Films for UA," *Boxoffice*, July 3, 1961, 6.
32. Broccoli, *When the Snow Melts*, 157.
33. "High Court of Justice," *The Times*, March 25, 1961, 12.
34. David V. Picker, *Musts, Maybes, and Nevers: A Book about the Movies* (North Charleston, SC: CreateSpace Independent Publishing Platform, 2013), 43.
35. Balio, *United Artists*, 230.
36. Picker, *Musts, Maybes and Nevers*, 52.
37. Financing agreement between Danjaq SA and United Artists Corporation, April 10, 1962, Film Finances Archive, Realised Film Box 328: *Dr No*.
38. Robert Sellers, *The Battle for Bond: The Genesis of Cinema's Greatest Hero* (Sheffield, UK: Tomahawk Press, 2007), 117–22.
39. Financing agreement between Danjaq SA and United Artists Corporation, April 10, 1962.
40. Ian Fleming to Norman Felton, July 16, 1963, Norman Felton Papers, University of Iowa Special Collections, https://digital.lib.uiowa.edu/islandora/object/ui%3Arescoll_90, accessed September 2, 2021.
41. See Cynthia W. Walker, "*The Man from U.N.C.L.E.*: Ian Fleming's Other Spy," in *James Bond in World and Popular Culture: The Films Are Not Enough*, ed. Robert G. Weiner, B. Lynn Whitfield, and Jack Becker (Newcastle: Cambridge Scholars, 2010), 235–51.
42. Broccoli, *When the Snow Melts*, 169.
43. Robert Garrett to Eon Productions, December 18, 1961, Film Finances Archive, Realised Film Box 328: *Dr No*.

44. "Greater Flexibility in Booking Is Needed, Says F. L. Thomas," *Kinematograph Weekly*, 30 May 1963, 95.
45. Mort Nathanson to Sam Kneider, January 9, 1962, United Artists Collection, MCHC 82-046 Box 3, Folder 4: *Dr. No*, Wisconsin Historical Society, Center for Film and Theater Research, University of Wisconsin–Madison (hereafter Wisconsin/UA).
46. Jonathan Bignell, "Pinter, Authorship and Entrepreneurship in 1960s British Cinema: The Economics of *The Quiller Memorandum*," *Historical Journal of Film, Radio, and Television* 40, no. 3 (2020): 533–50.
47. George Ornstein to Ilya Lopert, October 25, 1962, Wisconsin/UA: *Dr. No*.
48. Mark Glancy, *Cary Grant: The Making of a Hollywood Legend* (Oxford: Oxford University Press, 2020), 381.
49. Edward Biddulph, "The Original Model Bond," *MI6: The Home of James Bond 007*, April 5, 2013, https://www.mi6-hq.com/sections/articles/history_dr_no_casting_peter_anthony.php3 (accessed 02.09.2021).
50. "James Bond Thrillers to Be Filmed," *The Daily Gleaner*, July 21, 1961, 6.
51. Broccoli, *When the Snow Melts*, 164–65, 169–70.
52. George Ornstein to David Picker, September 18, 1961, Wisconsin/United Artists: *Dr No*.
53. "Scots Actor in Star Role," *Liverpool Echo*, November 3, 1961, 9.
54. Ian Fleming to Blanche Blackwell, October 25, 1961, in *The Man with the Golden Typewriter: Ian Fleming's James Bond Letters*, ed. Fergus Fleming (London: Bloomsbury, 2015), 257.
55. Broccoli, *When the Snow Melts*, 161–62.
56. Balio, *United Artists*, 258.
57. John Croydon to Robert Garrett, August 29, 1956, Film Finances Archive, Realised Film Box 192: *Action of the Tiger*.
58. Picker, *Musts, Maybes and Nevers*, 46.
59. Richard Schenkman, "The Terence Young Interview," *Bondage* 10 (1981), 2.
60. Harry Saltzman to George Ornstein, December 12, 1961, Wisconsin/UA: *Dr No*.
61. John Croydon to Robert Garrett, December 16, 1961, Film Finances Archive, Realised Film Box 328: *Dr No*.
62. Robert Garrett to Eon Productions, December 18, 1961, Film Finances Archive, Realised Film Box 328: *Dr No*.
63. Saltzman to Ornstein, December 12, 1961.

64. Harry Saltzman to Film Finances, December 29, 1961, Film Finances Archive, Realised Film Box 328: *Dr No*. The increased budget was confirmed by Stanley Sopel on January 1, 1962.

3. MONKEY BUSINESS

1. Albert R. Broccoli, with Donald Zec, *When the Snow Melts: The Autobiography of Cubby Broccoli* (London: Boxtree, 1998), 158.
2. "Richard Maibaum: A Pretense of Seriousness," in *Backstory: Interviews with Screenwriters of Hollywood's Golden Age*, ed. Pat McGilligan (Berkeley: University of California Press, 1986), 284.
3. Richard Schenkman, "The Terence Young Interview," *Bondage* 10 (1981), 7.
4. Matthew Field, "The Girl with the Golden Pen," *Cinema Retro: Dr. No: Movie Classics Special #4* (2012), 136–38.
5. Field, "Girl with the Golden Pen," 138.
6. Final Production Budget, Film Finances Archive, Realised Film Box 328: *Dr. No*.
7. *Kine Weekly*, July 27 1961, 13.
8. "Doctor No-No," *The Stage*, June 10, 1999, 9.
9. Adrian Turner, *Goldfinger*, Bloomsbury Movie Guide No. 2 (London: Bloomsbury, 1998), 130.
10. Richard Maibaum, "James Bond's 39 Bumps," *New York Times*, December 13, 1964, X9.
11. "Ian Fleming's Thunderball," screenplay by Richard Maibaum, August 18, 1961, collection of Gary J. Firuta.
12. Untitled manuscript article on the Bond films by Richard Maibaum, undated but ca. late 1965/early 1966, Richard Maibaum Papers MSC0149 (hereafter Iowa/Maibaum), Box 34, University of Iowa Special Collections.
13. "Doctor No: A Film Treatment by Richard Maibaum and Wolf Mankowitz. Based on the novel by Ian Fleming," September 7, 1961, Iowa/Maibaum, Box 20.
14. "Doctor No: A Film Treatment by Richard Maibaum and Wolf Mankowitz," revised September 25, 1961, Iowa/Maibaum, Box 20.
15. Klaus Dodds, "Screening Geopolitics: James Bond and the Early Cold War films (1962–1967)," *Geopolitics* 10, no. 2 (2005): 266–89.
16. Andrew Lycett, *Ian Fleming* (London: Weidenfeld and Nicolson, 1995), 367–68.

3. MONKEY BUSINESS

17. Dodds, "Screening Geopolitics," 276.
18. Although the Chinese connection would not be maintained in the finished film, Red China would feature in other early Bond movies. In *Goldfinger* (1964), the Chinese government supplies the title villain with an atomic bomb to destroy the US gold bullion depository at Fort Knox; Chinese or possibly North Korean agents are behind SPECTRE's attempt to trigger a war between the United States and the Soviet Union in *You Only Live Twice* (1967).
19. "Dr. No," screenplay by Richard Maibaum and Wolf Mankowitz, October 3, 1961, Iowa/Maibaum, Box 20.
20. George Ornstein to David Picker, October 6, 1961, United Artists Collection, MCHC82–046, Box 3, Folder 4: *Dr. No*, Wisconsin Historical Society, Center for Film and Theater Research, University of Wisconsin–Madison (hereafter Wisconsin/UA).
21. Fourth Draft Screenplay by Richard Maibaum and Wolf Mankowitz, December 12, 1961, Unpublished Script S6500: "Dr. No: From the Novel by Ian Fleming," British Film Institute Library.
22. Broccoli, *When the Snow Melts*, 183.
23. David Picker to Broccoli and Saltzman, January 15, 1963, Wisconsin/UA MCHC82–046, Box 3, Folder 6: *From Russia with Love*.
24. Kingsley Amis, *The James Bond Dossier* (London: Jonathan Cape, 1965), 89.
25. Amis, *James Bond Dossier*, 46.
26. "007's Oriental Eyefuls," *Playboy*, June 1967, 86.
27. Fifth Draft Screenplay by Richard Maibaum, Wolf Mankowitz, and J. M. Harwood, January 8, 1962, Unpublished Script S18574, "Ian Fleming's Dr. No," British Film Institute Library.
28. "Some Are Born Great," *Nursery World*, September 3, 1959, 11.
29. Melanie Williams, "Her Word Was Her Bond: Johanna Harwood, Bond's First Woman Screenwriter," in *From Blofeld to Moneypenny: Gender in James Bond*, ed. Steven Gerrard (Bingley, UK: Emerald, 2020), 124.
30. George Ornstein to David Picker, December 12, 1961, Wisconsin/UA: *Dr. No*.
31. *The Sunday Times*, November 20, 1960, 27.
32. Field, "Girl with the Golden Pen," 138.
33. Schenkman, "Terence Young Interview," 2.
34. Tracy Hargreaves, "The Trevelyan Years: British Censorship and 1960s Cinema," in *Behind the Scenes at the BBFC: Film Classification from the*

4. UNDERNEATH THE MANGO TREE

Silver Screen to the Digital Age, ed. Edward Lamberti (London: Palgrave Macmillan/British Film Institute, 2012), 55.
35. "£140,000 Goya Vanishes," *The Times*, August 23, 1961, 8.
36. "Dr. No and the Goya," *The Sunday Times*, October 7, 1962, 27; "That Goya Joke," *The Sunday Times*, October 21, 1962, 42; "More Goya Jokers," *The Sunday Times*, November 4, 1962, 38.
37. *Daily Express*, October 5, 1962.
38. *The Spectator*, October 12, 1962.
39. Penelope Houston, "007," *Sight & Sound* 34, no. 1 (Winter 1964–1965): 15.

4. UNDERNEATH THE MANGO TREE

1. Unit Progress Report No. 1, January 16, 1962, Film Finances Archive, Realised Film Box 328: *Dr. No*.
2. "Merry-Go-Round," *The Daily Gleaner*, January 22, 1962, 6.
3. "Jamaicans in 'Dr. No,'" *The Daily Gleaner*, September 11, 1963, 6.
4. "'Dr. No' team Arrives," *The Daily Gleaner*, January 16, 1962, 6.
5. "Red Tape Again," *The Daily Gleaner*, February 20, 1962, 10.
6. James Robertson, "Rewriting *Dr. No* in 1962: James Bond and the End of the British Empire in Jamaica," *Small Axe* 19, no. 2 (2015): 61.
7. John Pearson, *The Life of Ian Fleming* (London: Jonathan Cape, 1966), 333.
8. Ian Fleming to Blanche Blackwell, October 25, 1961, in *The Man with the Golden Typewriter: Ian Fleming's James Bond Letters*, ed. Fergus Fleming (London: Bloomsbury, 2015), 256–57.
9. "London Diary," *The Sunday Times*, December 3, 1961, 6.
10. Matthew Parker, *Goldeneye: Where Bond Was Born: Ian Fleming's Jamaica* (London: Hutchinson, 2014), 277–78.
11. Mort Nathanson to Sam Kreisler, January 9, 1962, United Artists Collection, MCHC82–046, Box 3, Folder 4: *Dr. No*, Wisconsin Historical Society, Center for Film and Theater Research, University of Wisconsin–Madison (hereafter Wisconsin/UA).
12. Irma Bunt points out Andress to Bond (in mufti as Sir Hilary Bray) in the public restaurant at Piz Gloria: "And that beautiful girl with the long fair hair at the big table, that is Ursula Andress, the film star. What a wonderful tan she has!" Ian Fleming, *On Her Majesty's Secret Service* (London: Penguin Classics, 2004 [1963]), 118.
13. Ann Fleming to Evelyn Waugh, February 17, 1962, in *The Letters of Ann Fleming*, ed. Mark Amory (London: Collins, 1985), 297–98.

4. UNDERNEATH THE MANGO TREE

14. Daily Production Reports No. 22 (February 9, 1962) and 23 (February 10 1963), Film Finances Archive: *Dr. No*.
15. Andrew Lycett, *Ian Fleming* (London: Weidenfeld & Nicolson, 1995), 399.
16. Film Finances to Eon Productions, February 12, 1962, Film Finances Archive: *Dr. No*.
17. Harry Saltzman to Robert Garrett, February 18, 1962, Film Finances Archive: *Dr. No*.
18. J. A. H. Duffins to Eon Productions, April 21, 1962, Film Finances Archive: *Dr. No*.
19. "Dr. No: Summary of location shooting," March 29, 1962, Film Finances Archive: *Dr. No*.
20. Terence Young to Hans Marcus, May 3, 1962, Film Finances Archive: *Dr. No*.
21. Robert Garrett to Peter Hope, "Notes on Terence Young," no date, Film Finances Archive: *Dr. No*.
22. Ken Adam to Film Finances, December 22, 1961, Film Finances Archive: *Dr. No*.
23. Ken Adam to Harry Saltzman, February 1, 1962, Film Finances Archive: *Dr. No*.
24. Commentary track for *Dr. No: Special 007 Edition* (MGM/UA Home Entertainment, DVD 16168, 2008).
25. Saltzman had previous form for using his contingency fund to enhance production values. See James Chapman, "The Trouble with Harry: The Difficult Relationship of Harry Saltzman and Film Finances," *Historical Journal of Film, Radio, and Television* 34, no. 1 (2014): 43–71.
26. Studio Progress Report No. 1, February 26, 1962, Film Finances Archive: *Dr. No*.
27. "Notes on Terence Young."
28. "Dr. No–Studio," no date, Film Finances Archive: *Dr. No*.
29. Richard Schenkman, "The Terence Young Interview," *Bondage* 10 (1981): 9.
30. Eunice Gayson, with Andrew Boyle and Gareth Owen, *The First Lady of Bond* (London: Signum Books, 2012), 150–51.
31. Studio Progress Report No. 5, March 2, 1962, Film Finances Archive: *Dr. No*.
32. Bernard Smith to Colin Crewe (Tufnell, Satterthwaite & Co.), March 16, 1962, Film Finances Archive: *Dr. No*.
33. Robert Garrett to Harry Saltzman, March 16, 1962, Film Finances Archive: *Dr. No*.

4. UNDERNEATH THE MANGO TREE

34. Saltzman to Garrett, March 29, 1962, Film Finances Archive: *Dr. No.*
35. Bernard Smith to Tufnell, Satterthwaite & Co., no date, Film Finances Archive: *Dr. No.*
36. The first occasion on which Film Finances had exercised its takeover option was *The Gift Horse* (Jay Lewis Productions, 1952) where a breakdown in communication between the producer and director led to Film Finances firing the producer. Others included *Action of the Tiger* (MGM/Claridge Productions, 1957), directed by Terence Young, and *The Valiant* (United Artists/BHP Films, 1962), both of which had gone significantly over budget on location. Film Finances threatened to but in the end did not take over Saltzman's *The Iron Petticoat* (1956) when it emerged after completion—and after Film Finances had paid coproducer Betty Box a "no-claim bonus"—that Saltzman had left bills unpaid.
37. Robert Garrett to Harry Saltzman, April 3, 1962, Film Finances Archive: *Dr. No.*
38. Garrett to Bernard Smith, April 10, 1962, Film Finances Archive: *Dr. No.*
39. "Estimated cost of Shots required to complete as per schedule," April 18, 1962, Film Finances Archive: *Dr. No.*"
40. Studio Progress Report No. 28, April 26, 1962, Film Finances Archive: *Dr. No.*
41. Garrett to Saltzman, April 10, 1962, Film Finances Archive: *Dr. No.*
42. Statement of production cost for week ending 10 March 1962, Film Finances Archive: *Dr. No.*
43. Final production cost of *Dr. No*, audited by Nyman Libson, Paul & Co. (chartered accountants), December 11, 1962, Film Finances Archive: *Dr. No.*
44. Bernard Lewis to Colin Crewe, May 11, 1962, Film Finances Archive: *Dr. No.*
45. Garrett to Saltzman, April 25, 1962, Film Finances Archive: *Dr. No.*
46. Letter of agreement between Danjaq SA and Film Finances, April 10, 1962, Film Finances Archive: *Dr. No.*
47. There were eight separate advances from Film Finances to the *Dr. No* production account: £20,000 (April 16, 1962), £17,000 (May 8), £1,500 (May 18), £2,500 (May 25), £2,000 (August 3), £240 (August 10), £3,700 (August 17), and £750 (August 24).
48. Robert Garrett to Fineo Limited, August 30, 1962, Film Finances Archive: *Dr. No.*
49. "Dr. No: Production Advances making up Final Cost," January 11, 1963, Film Finances Archive: *Dr. No.*

50. Memorandum: "United Artists," January 23, 1963, Film Finances Archive, General Correspondence, Box 31.
51. George Ornstein to Sidney Landan, January 31, 1963, Wisconsin/UA, MCHC82–046 Box 3 f.6: *From Russia with Love*.
52. R. S. Aikin to Bernard Smith, February 8, 1963, Film Finances Archive: *Dr. No*.
53. Robert Garrett to Peter Hope, August 15, 1962, Film Finances Archive: *Dr. No*.
54. Garrett to Aikin, October 31, 1962, Film Finances Archive: *Dr. No*.
55. "Your Films," *Kine Weekly*, October 11, 1962, 14; October 18, 1962, 11; November 1, 1962, 9.
56. Preliminary report on budget overcost, June 8, 1961, Film Finances Archive, Realised Film Box 311: *The Valiant*.
57. Certified final cost of production by Nyman Libson, Paul & Co., July 31, 1963, Film Finances Archive, Realised Film Box 339: *Lancelot and Guinevere*.
58. Universal Pictures' statement of Emblem Productions re: *Sword of Lancelot* to 27 September 1980, Film Finances Archive, Realised Film Box 339: *Lancelot and Guinevere*. By this time, the "total accountable gross" amounted to US$2,592,827.
59. Memorandum: "Tom Jones," September 27, 1962, Film Finances Archive, Realised Film Box 346: *Tom Jones*.
60. Deed of Variation between Woodfall Film Productions and Film Finances, February 22, 1963, Film Finances Archive, Realised Film Box 346: *Tom Jones*.
61. Memorandum: "United Artists," January 23, 1963, Film Finances Archive, General Correspondence, Box 31.
62. Robert Garrett to Alessandro Tasca, September 21, 1962, Film Finances Archive, General Correspondence, Box 101.
63. Arnold Picker to Bill Bernstein, March 30, 1964, Wisconsin/UA, MCHC82–046, Box 3, Folder 11: *Goldfinger*.
64. Film Finances to Danjaq, November 4, 1964, Film Finances Archive, General Correspondence, Box 76.
65. David V. Picker, *Musts, Maybes, and Nevers: A Book About the Movies* (North Charleston, SC: CreateSpace Independent Publishing Platform, 2013), 17–18.
66. Robert Garrett to George Ornstein, May 22, 1963, Film Finances Archive, General Correspondence, Box 31.

5. A BIZARRE COMEDY MELODRAMA

67. Robert Garrett to Eon Productions, July 24, 1963, Film Finances Archive: *Dr. No*.
68. W. J. Smith to Bernard Smith, October 9, 1963, Film Finances Archive: *Dr. No*.
69. Distribution statement to February 29, 1964, Film Finances Archive: *Dr. No*.
70. Tino Balio, *United Artists*, Volume 2: *1951–1978: The Company That Changed the Film Industry* (Madison: University of Wisconsin Press, 1987), 261.
71. "'Goldfinger' Projects over $20-Mil," *Variety*, February 16, 1965, 3.
72. Picker, *Musts, Maybes, and Nevers*, 52.
73. "007 Pix Rentals Hit $100,000," *Variety*, October 12, 1966, 1.

5. A BIZARRE COMEDY MELODRAMA

1. "Harry Saltzman Recalls Early Coolness to Bond Features," *Variety*, May 11, 1987, 80.
2. Alexander Walker, *Hollywood, England: The British Film Industry in the 1960s* (London: Michael Joseph, 1974), 189.
3. George Ornstein to David Picker, February 9, 1962, United Artists Collection, MCHC82–046, Box 3, Folder 4: *Dr. No*, Wisconsin Historical Society, Center for Film and Theater Research, University of Wisconsin–Madison (hereafter Wisconsin/UA).
4. Charles Juroe to Fred Goldberg, March 23, 1962, Wisconsin/UA, MCHC82–046, Box 3, Folder 4: *Dr. No*.
5. Harry Saltzman to Robert Garrett, 29 March 1962, Film Finances Archive, Realised Film Box 328: *Dr. No*.
6. Memorandum–"United Artists," January 23, 1963, Film Finances Archive, General Correspondence, Box 31.
7. *The Daily Cinema*, September 4, 1962, 6.
8. *Kine Weekly*, September 6, 1962, 16.
9. *Variety*, November 17, 1962, 6.
10. *Daily Mirror*, October 5, 1962, 25.
11. *Topic*, October 6, 1962.
12. *Evening Standard*, October 4, 1962.
13. *Daily Herald*, October 6, 1962, 6.
14. *Daily Express*, October 5, 1962.
15. *Daily Mail*, October 5, 1962, 16.
16. *The Sunday Times*, October 7, 1962, 41.

5. A BIZARRE COMEDY MELODRAMA

17. *Punch*, October 17, 1962, 25–6.
18. *Financial Times*, October 5, 1962, 26.
19. *The Observer*, October 7, 1962.
20. *The New Statesman*, October 9, 1962.
21. *The Guardian*, October 6, 1962, 5.
22. *The Times*, October 5, 1962, 18.
23. *Monthly Film Bulletin*, October 1962, 156.
24. *Sight & Sound* 31, no. 4 (Autumn 1962): 197.
25. *Amateur Cine World*, November 8, 1962, 691.
26. *The People*, October 7, 1962, 16.
27. *The Spectator*, October 12, 1962.
28. *Daily Worker*, October 6, 1962.
29. *Sunday Express*, October 7, 1962.
30. *Films and Filming* 9, no. 2 (November 1962): 36.
31. "Your Films," *Kine Weekly*, October 11, 1962, 14.
32. *The Daily Cinema*, October 10, 1962, 2.
33. "Your Films," *Kine Weekly*, November 1, 1962, 9.
34. "Three British Films Head the General Releases," *Kine Weekly*, December 13, 1962, 7.
35. "The Top Ten of '62: 'Films and Filming' Names Money-Makers," *The Daily Cinema*, December 10, 1962, 5.
36. Quoted in John Francis Lane, "Young Romantic," *Films and Filming* 13, no. 5 (February 1967): 58.
37. J. Hoberman, "When Dr. No Met Dr. Strangelove," *Sight & Sound*, New Series 3, no. 12 (December 1993): 18.
38. Lane, "Young Romantic," 58.
39. On the historical moment of the new wave, see Arthur Marwick, "*Room at the Top, Saturday Night and Sunday Morning*, and the 'Cultural Revolution' in Britain," *Journal of Contemporary British History* 19, no. 1 (1984): 127–52.
40. "Changes Continue in British Industry," *Boxoffice*, April 15, 1963, 106A.
41. Linda Wood, ed., *BFI Information Guide 1: British Film Industry* (London: British Film Institute Information and Education Department, 1980), Appendix A (unpaginated).
42. Asa Briggs, *The History of Broadcasting in the United Kingdom*, Volume V: *Competition: 1955–1974* (Oxford: Oxford University Press, 1995), 1005.
43. *The Illustrated London News*, October 27, 1962, 672.
44. *The Daily Cinema*, November 26, 1962, 1.

5. A BIZARRE COMEDY MELODRAMA

45. Tony Bennett and Janet Woollacott, *Bond and Beyond: The Political Career of a Popular Hero* (London: Macmillan, 1987), 26.
46. Ian Fleming, "How to Write a Thriller," *Books and Bookmen*, May 1963, 19.
47. Quoted in "No, No, a Thousand Times No," *Time*, October 19, 1962.
48. *The Hollywood Reporter*, March 15, 1963, 3.
49. *Film Daily*, March 19, 1963, 7.
50. *Independent Exhibitors Film Bulletin*, March 18, 1963, 18.
51. *The Motion Picture Herald*, April 3, 1963, 785.
52. *Boxoffice*, April 1, 1963, 2717.
53. *New York Times*, May 30, 1963, 15.
54. *Washington Post*, May 23, 1963, A30.
55. *The Saturday Review*, June 1, 1963 (BFI clippings).
56. *New Yorker*, June 1, 1963, 65.
57. *New Republic*, June 15, 1966, 36.
58. *Time*, May 31, 1963, 80.
59. Albert R. Broccoli, with Donald Zec, *When the Snow Melts: The Autobiography of Cubby Broccoli* (London: Boxtree, 1998), 177–78.
60. Halsey Raines to Sam Friedman, February 15, 1962, Wisconsin/UA: *Dr. No*.
61. "UA Selling Campaign on Its 'Dr. No' Film," *Boxoffice*, February 25, 1963, 10.
62. Charles Juroe to Fred Goldberg, March 23, 1962, Wisconsin/UA: *Dr. No*.
63. "450 Situations Play 'Dr. No' at Opening," *Variety*, April 3, 1963, 19.
64. "New York Says 'Yes,'" *Boxoffice*, June 10, 1963, 6.
65. "'Dr. No's Three Weeks of Yes-Yes Public Reaction via 'Premiere Showcase,'" *Variety*, June 26, 1963, 26.
66. *Boxoffice*, September 30, 1963, 156; August 19, 1963, 132; November 25, 1963, 188; September 2, 1963, 140; August 5, 1963, 124.
67. "Top Rental Films of 1963," *Variety*, January 8, 1964, 67.
68. "Big Rental Pictures of 1964," *Variety*, January 6, 1965, 39.
69. "Big Rental Pictures of 1965," *Variety*, January 5, 1966, 6.
70. "United Artists' Fort Knox," *Variety*, March 31, 1965, 3.
71. "United Artists 60% Terms When Reissuing 'Goldfinger' with 'Dr. No,'" *Variety*, May 18, 1966, 3.
72. "Holiday Boosts B'way; 'No'-'Russia' Giant $82,000," *Variety*, June 2, 1965, 9.
73. "'Dr. No,' 'From Russia with Love' Open San Francisco with 400," *Boxoffice*, May 31, 1965, W6.

5. A BIZARRE COMEDY MELODRAMA

74. *Boxoffice*, September 27, 1965, 150.
75. *Boxoffice*, October 17, 1966, 160.
76. John Sedgwick, *Changing to Stay the Same: Hollywood, 1946 to 1965*, Discussion Papers in Business Economics 31 (London: University of North London, 2001), 5.
77. Sedgwick, *Changing to Stay the Same*, 8.
78. "United Artists' Fort Knox," 3.
79. Paul Monaco, *History of the American Cinema: The Sixties: 1960–1969* (Berkeley: University of California Press, 2001), 193–94.
80. The Margaret Herrick Library at the Academy of Motion Picture Arts and Sciences, Los Angeles, holds the records of the Production Code Administration. The file on *Dr. No* does not include any script or correspondence. The film was approved on November 14, 1962. For *From Russia with Love*, the PCA accepted the same cuts that had been made by the British Board of Film Censors. These related mostly to sex references, the performance of the belly dancer, and an implied nude shot of Tatiana.
81. "Proposed New Code Raises Issue of 'Adult' Definition, Artistic Merit," *Variety*, August 24, 1966, 30.
82. "James Bond: The Films with the Golden Touch," *Hollywood Reporter*, July 14, 1987, S-26.
83. "Bond Box-Office Grosses," *Screen International*, November 17, 1995, 38.
84. "Kingston Premiere for *Dr. No*," *The Daily Gleaner*, January 28, 1963, 18.
85. "James Bond Starts New Film Trend," *The Sunday Gleaner*, November 1, 1964, 16.
86. "ABC Bottled in Bond; 7 Pix Big Payout," *Variety*, July 5, 1972, 27.
87. "007 goes to ITV in a Record £850,000 Deal," *Daily Mail*, October 28, 1975, 19.
88. "*Dr. No* Pays Off with 10 Million Homes Ratings Bonus," *Broadcast*, November 17, 1975, 4.

6. I'M JUST LOOKING

1. The script opens with the three blind beggars walking along King Street in downtown Kingston. The superimposed titles would begin as they cross the road and continue over a series of dissolves as the men make their way along Harbour Street and through Victoria Market, ending as they

6. I'M JUST LOOKING

arrive outside Queen's Club. Fifth Draft Screenplay by Richard Maibaum, Wolf Mankowitz, and J. M. Harwood, January 8, 1962, British Film Institute Library, Unpublished Script S18574: *Ian Fleming's Dr. No*.

2. Maurice Binder, "How I Designed the Titles for *Dr. No*," *Amateur Movie-Maker* 6, no. 2 (February 1963): 70.
3. The term "Structural Film"—which later developed into "Structural-Materialist Film"—was coined by P. Adams Sitney to describe experimental work by filmmakers such as Ted Conrad, Hollis Frampton, Paul Sharits, Michael Snow, and Joyce Weiland in the 1960s. Its characteristics include a fixed camera, flicker effects, loop printing, and rephotography. The films were usually shown as part of art installations in galleries and workshops. See P. Adams Sitney, *Visionary Film: The American Avant-Garde, 1943–2000*, 3rd edition (New York: Oxford University Press, 2002), 347–72.
4. Jan-Christopher Horak, "Branding 007: Title Sequences in the James Bond Films," in *The Cultural Life of James Bond: Specters of 007*, ed. Jaap Verheul (Amsterdam: Amsterdam University Press, 2020), 252.
5. The term "cinema of attractions" was coined by film historian Tom Gunning to describe the period between 1895 and 1906, before narrative film became dominant. See Tom Gunning, "The Cinema of Attractions: Early Film, Its Spectator and the Avant-Garde," in *Early Cinema: Space, Frame, Narrative*, ed. Thomas Elsaesser (London: British Film Institute, 1990), 56–62.
6. Pat Kirkham, "Dots & Sickles," *Sight & Sound* n.s. 5, no. 12 (December 1995): 11.
7. Christopher Holliday, "Bond and Art Cinema," in *The Cultural Life of James Bond*, 242–43.
8. Brian O'Doherty, "A Vivid Art Season," *New York Times*, December 27, 1962, 5.
9. David Buxton, *From* The Avengers *to* Miami Vice*: Form and Ideology in Television Series* (Manchester: Manchester University Press, 1990), 76–77.
10. Laurie N. Ede, *British Film Design: A History* (London: I. B. Tauris, 2010), 119–23.
11. Quoted in Christopher Frayling, *Ken Adam: The Art of Production Design* (London: Faber and Faber, 2005), 95.
12. Quoted in Frayling, *Ken Adam*, 96.
13. Quoted in Frayling, *Ken Adam*, 98.

6. I'M JUST LOOKING

14. See Andrew Higson, "Space, Place, Spectacle: Landscape and Townscape in the 'Kitchen Sink' Film," in *Dissolving Views: Key Writings on British Cinema*, ed. Andrew Higson (London: Cassell, 1996), 133–56.
15. Duncan Petrie, *The British Cinematographer* (London: British Film Institute, 1996), 123.
16. Umberto Eco, "The Narrative Structure in Fleming," in *The Bond Affair*, ed. Oreste Del Buono and Umberto Eco, trans. R. A. Downie (London: Macdonald, 1966), 39.
17. Eco, "Narrative Structure in Fleming," 58.
18. Eco, "Narrative Structure in Fleming," 52.
19. Buxton, *From* The Avengers *to* Miami Vice, 77.
20. Andrew Rissik, *The James Bond Man: The Films of Sean Connery* (London: Elm Tree, 1983), 50.
21. *30 Years of James Bond* (London Weekend Television for ITV, prod. Lorna Dickinson, October 3, 1992. On the tailoring of Connery's Bond in *Dr. No*, see Llewella Chapman, *Fashioning James Bond: Costume, Gender and Identity in the World of 007* (London: Bloomsbury, 2022), 9–32.
22. Albert R. Broccoli, with Donald Zec, *When the Snow Melts: The Autobiography of Cubby Broccoli* (London: Boxtree, 1998), 171.
23. Sue Harper, *Women in British Cinema: Mad, Bad and Dangerous to Know* (London: Continuum, 2000), 119.
24. Claire Hines, *The Playboy and James Bond: 007, Ian Fleming and "Playboy" Magazine* (Manchester: Manchester University Press, 2018), 131.
25. Richard Schenkman, "The Terence Young Interview," *Bondage* 10 (1981): 9.
26. Fifth Draft Screenplay.
27. Laura Mulvey, "Visual Pleasure and Narrative Cinema," *Screen* 16, no. 3 (1975): 11.
28. While this is not the place for an extended discussion of the theoretical implications of Mulvey's article, it should be mentioned that its assumption of a heteronormative male spectator has subsequently been challenged (including by the author herself). Later Bond films have subverted the idea of gendered spectatorship: the Daniel Craig films—most explicitly *Casino Royale* (2006)—have demonstrated a tendency to display Bond's body as spectacle for the gratification of both heterosexual female and gay male spectators.
29. Ian Fleming, *Dr. No* (London: Penguin Classics, 2004 [1958]), 144.

CONCLUSION

30. John Hill, *Sex, Class and Realism: British Cinema, 1956–1963* (London: British Film Institute, 1986), 157.
31. Hill, *Sex, Class and Realism*, 174.
32. *Goldfinger* seems to me the most overtly misogynistic of the early Bond films: in it, two women—Jill Masterson (Shirley Eaton) and Tilly Masterson (Tania Mallet)—are murdered as a consequence of their involvement with Bond. The former's death (suffocated by gold paint) is treated in the film as a form of erotic spectacle.
33. Raymond Durgnat, *A Mirror for England: British Movies from Austerity to Affluence* (London: Faber and Faber, 1970), 151.
34. "Jamaicans in *Dr. No*," *The Daily Gleaner*, September 11, 1963, 6.
35. James Robertson, "Rewriting *Dr. No* in 1962: James Bond and the End of the British Empire in Jamaica," *Small Axe* 19, no. 2 (2015): 56.
36. "A Man to Meet," *The Daily Gleaner*, September 28, 1963, 6.
37. Chapman, *Fashioning James Bond*, 24–25.
38. Anna Everett, "Shaken, Not Stirred Britishness: James Bond, Race, and the Transnational Imaginary," in *The Cultural Life of James Bond*, 192.

CONCLUSION

1. Andrew Sarris, *The American Cinema: Directors and Directions, 1929–1968* (New York: Da Capo Press, 1998 [1968]), 268.
2. Larry Gross, "Big and Loud," *Sight & Sound*, New Series 5, no. 8 (August 1995): 8.
3. *30 Years of James Bond*, London Weekend Television for ITV, prod. Lorna Dickinson, October 3, 1992.

BIBLIOGRAPHY

PRIMARY SOURCES—including archival documents, unpublished scripts, publicity materials, press reports, and contemporary reviews—can be traced through the endnotes.

I have used the UK Penguin Classics editions of the Bond books for reference. Note that the Penguin editions of *Dr. No* incorrectly identify the original Jonathan Cape publication as 1957 rather than 1958.

■ ■ ■

Adams, Alex. "'The Sweet Tang of Rape': Torture, Survival, and Masculinity in Ian Fleming's Bond Novels." *Feminist Theory* 18, no. 2 (2017): 137–58.
Albrecht, Donald. "Dr. Caligari's Cabinets: The Set Design of Ken Adam." In *Architecture and Film*, ed. Mark Lamster, 117–28. New York: Princeton Architectural Press, 2000.
Aldgate, Anthony. *Censorship and the Permissive Society: British Cinema and Theatre, 1955–1965*. Oxford: Clarendon Press, 1995.
Amis, Kingsley. *The James Bond Dossier*. London: Jonathan Cape, 1965.

BIBLIOGRAPHY

Amory, Mark, ed. *The Letters of Ann Fleming*. London: Collins, 1985.

Anez, Nicholas. "James Bond." *Films in Review* 18, no. 9–10 (September–October 1992): 311–19.

Armes, Roy. *A Critical History of the British Cinema*. London: Secker & Warburg, 1978.

Balio, Tino. *United Artists*. Volume 2: *1951–1978: The Company That Changed the Film Industry*. Madison: University of Wisconsin Press, 1987.

Barron, Cynthia. "*Doctor No*: Bonding Britishness to Racial Sovereignty." *Spectator: The University of Southern California Journal of Film and Television* 14, no. 2 (1994): 68–81.

Bennett, Tony, and Janet Woollacott. *Bond and Beyond: The Political Career of a Popular Hero*. London: Macmillan, 1987.

Benson, Raymond. *The James Bond Bedside Companion*. London: Boxtree, 1988.

Bertens, Hans. "A Society of Murderers Run on Sound Conservative Lines: The Life and Times of Sapper's Bulldog Drummond." In *Twentieth-Century Suspense: The Thriller Comes of Age*, ed. Clive Bloom, 51–68. London: Macmillan, 1990.

Bignell, Jonathan. "Pinter, Authorship, and Entrepreneurship in 1960s British Cinema: The Economics of *The Quiller Memorandum*." *Historical Journal of Film, Radio and Television* 40. no. 3 (2020): 533–50.

Black, Jeremy. *The Politics of James Bond: From Fleming's Novels to the Big Screen*. Westport, CT: Praeger, 2001.

Booker, Christopher. *The Neophiliacs: A Study of the Revolution in English Life in the Fifties and Sixties*. London: Collins, 1969.

Briggs, Asa. *The History of Broadcasting in the United Kingdom*. Volume V: *Competition: 1955–1974*. Oxford: Oxford University Press, 1995.

Broccoli, Albert R., with Donald Zec. *When the Snow Melts: The Autobiography of Cubby Broccoli*. London: Boxtree, 1998.

Brosnan, John. *James Bond in the Cinema*. London: Tantivy Press, 1972.

Buxton, David. *From* The Avengers *to* Miami Vice*: Form and Ideology in Television Series*. Manchester: Manchester University Press, 1990.

Cannadine, David. "James Bond and the Decline of England." *Encounter* 53, no. 3 (1979): 46–55.

Cawelti, John G. *Adventure, Mystery and Romance: Formula Stories as Art and Popular Culture*. Chicago: University of Chicago Press, 1976.

Chancellor, Henry. *James Bond: The Man and His World: The Official Companion to Ian Fleming's Creation*. London: John Murray, 2005.

BIBLIOGRAPHY

Chapman, James, "The Trouble with Harry: The Difficult Relationship of Harry Saltzman and Film Finances." *Historical Journal of Film, Radio and Television* 34, no. 1 (2014): 43–71.

Chapman, Llewella. *Fashioning James Bond: Costume, Gender, and Identity in the World of 007.* London: Bloomsbury, 2022.

Coward, Noël. *The Letters of Noël Coward.* Edited by Barry Day. London: Bloomsbury, 2007.

Cumper, G. E. "Preliminary Analysis of Population Growth and Social Characteristics in Jamaica, 1943–66." *Social and Economic Studies* 12, no. 4 (1963): 393–31.

Denning, Michael. *Cover Stories: Narrative and Ideology in the British Spy Thriller.* London: Routledge and Kegan Paul, 1987.

Dickinson, Margaret, and Sarah Street. *Cinema and State: The Film Industry and the British Government, 1927–84.* London: British Film Institute, 1985.

Dodds, Klaus. "Screening Geopolitics: James Bond and the Early Cold War Films (1962–1967)." *Geopolitics* 10, no. 2 (2005): 266–89.

Drazin, Charles. *A Bond for Bond: Film Finances and* Dr. No. London: Film Finances, 2012.

Duncan, Paul, ed. *The James Bond 007 Archives.* Cologne: Taschen, 2015.

Dunn, Anthony J. *The Worlds of Wolf Mankowitz: Between Elite and Popular Cultures in Post-War Britain.* Edgware: Vallentine Mitchell, 2013.

Durgnat, Raymond. *A Mirror for England: British Movies from Austerity to Affluence.* London: Faber and Faber, 1970.

Eco, Umberto. "The Narrative Structure in Fleming." In *The Bond Affair*, ed. Oreste Del Buono and Umberto Eco, trans. R. A. Downie, 35–75. London: Macdonald, 1966.

Ede, Laurie N. *British Film Design: A History.* London: I. B. Tauris, 2010.

Field, Matthew, and Ajay Chowdhury. *Some Kind of Hero: The Remarkable Story of the James Bond Films.* Stroud: The History Press, 2015.

Fleming, Fergus, ed. *The Man with the Golden Typewriter: Ian Fleming's James Bond Letters.* London: Bloomsbury, 2015.

Fleming, Ian. *Casino Royale.* London: Penguin Classics, 2004 [1953].

———. *Dr. No.* London: Penguin Classics, 2004 [1958].

———. *Goldfinger.* London: Penguin Classics, 2004 [1958].

———. "How to Write a Thriller." *Books and Bookmen*, May 1963, 14–19.

———. *Live and Let Die.* London: Penguin Classics, 2004 [1954].

———. *The Man with the Golden Gun.* London: Penguin Classics, 2006 [1965].

———. *Moonraker*. London: Penguin Classics, 2004 [1955].
———. *On Her Majesty's Secret Service*. London: Penguin Classics, 2004 [1963].
Frayling, Christopher. *Ken Adam: The Art of Production Design*. London: Faber and Faber, 2005.
Gayson, Eunice, with Andrew Boyle and Gareth Owen. *The First Lady of Bond*. London: Signum Books, 2012.
Glancy, Mark. *Cary Grant: The Making of a Hollywood Legend*. Oxford: Oxford University Press, 2020.
Gross, Larry. "Big and Loud." *Sight & Sound* n.s. 5, no. 8 (August 1995): 6–10.
Gunning, Tom. "The Cinema of Attractions: Early Film, Its Spectator and the Avant-Garde." In *Early Cinema: Space, Frame, Narrative*, ed. Thomas Elsaesser, 56–62. London: British Film Institute, 1990.
Hall, Sheldon. *Zulu: With Some Guts Behind It—The Making of the Epic Movie*. Sheffield: Tomahawk Press, 2005.
Halloran, Vivian. "Tropical Bond." In *Ian Fleming & James Bond: The Cultural Politics of 007*, ed. Edward P. Comentale, Stephen Watt, and Skip Willman, 158–77. Bloomington: Indiana University Press, 2005.
Hargreaves, Tracy. "The Trevelyan Years: British Censorship and 1960s Cinema." In *Behind the Scenes at the BBFC: Film Classification from the Silver Screen to the Digital Age*, ed. Edward Lamberti, 53–68. London: Bloomsbury/British Film Institute, 2012.
Harmetz, Aljean. *Round Up the Usual Suspects: The Making of* Casablanca: *Bogart, Bergman, and World War II*. London: Weidenfeld & Nicolson, 1993.
Harper, Sue. *Women in British Cinema: Mad, Bad and Dangerous to Know*. London: Continuum, 2000.
Higson, Andrew. "Space, Place, Spectacle: Landscape and Townscape in the 'Kitchen Sink' Film." In *Dissolving Views: Key Writings on British Cinema*, ed. Andrew Higson, 133–56. London: Cassell, 1996.
Hill, John. *Sex, Class and Realism: British Cinema, 1956–1963*. London: British Film Institute, 1986.
Hines, Claire. *The Playboy and James Bond: 007, Ian Fleming, and* Playboy *Magazine* Manchester: Manchester University Press, 2018.
Hoberman, J. "When Dr. No Met Dr. Strangelove." *Sight & Sound* n.s. 3, no. 12 (December 1993): 16–21.
Houston, Penelope. "007." *Sight & Sound* 14, no. 1 (Winter 1964–1965): 14–16.
Kirkham, Pat. "Dots & Sickles." *Sight & Sound* n.s. 5, no. 12 (December 1995): 10–12.

BIBLIOGRAPHY

Lane, John Stewart. "Young Romantic." *Films and Filming* 13, no. 5 (February 1967): 58–60.

Lane, Sheldon, ed. *For Bond Lovers Only*. London: Panther, 1965.

Lycett, Andrew. *Ian Fleming*. London: Weidenfeld & Nicolson, 1995.

Macintyre, Ben. *For Your Eyes Only: Ian Fleming + James Bond*. London: Bloomsbury, 2008.

Marwick, Arthur. "*Room at the Top, Saturday Night and Sunday Morning*, and the 'Cultural Revolution' in Britain." *Journal of Contemporary History* 19, no. 1 (1984): 127–52.

McGilligan, Pat, ed. *Backstory: Interviews with Writers of Hollywood's Golden Age*. Berkeley: University of California Press, 1986.

McKay, Sinclair. *The Man with the Golden Touch: How the Bond Films Conquered the World*. New York: Overlook Press, 2010.

Monaco, Paul. *History of the American Cinema: The Sixties: 1960–1969*. Berkeley: University of California Press, 2001.

Morgan, Kenneth O. *The People's Peace: British History, 1945–1990*. Oxford: Oxford University Press, 1992.

Mulvey, Laura. "Visual Pleasure and Narrative Cinema." *Screen* 16, no. 3 (1975): 6–18.

Osborne, John. *Looking Back: Never Explain, Never Apologise*. London: Faber and Faber, 1999.

Parker, Matthew. *Goldeneye: Where Bond Was Born: Ian Fleming's Jamaica*. London: Hutchinson, 2014.

Pearson, John. *The Life of Ian Fleming*. London: Jonathan Cape, 1966.

Petrie, Duncan. *The British Cinematographer*. London: British Film Institute, 1996.

Pfeiffer, Lee, and Philip Lisa. *The Incredible World of 007*. London: Boxtree, 1992.

Pfeiffer, Lee, and Dave Worrall. *The Essential Bond: The Authorized Guide to the World of 007*. London: Boxtree, 1998.

Picker, David V. *Musts, Maybes, and Nevers: A Book About the Movies*. North Charleston, SC: CreateSpace Independent Publishing Platform, 2013.

Richards, Jeffrey. *Films and British National Identity: From Dickens to* Dad's Army. Manchester: Manchester University Press, 1997.

Richardson, Tony. *Long-Distance Runner: A Memoir*. London: Faber and Faber, 1993.

Rissik, Andrew. *The James Bond Man: The Films of Sean Connery*. London: Elm Tree Press, 1983.

BIBLIOGRAPHY

Robertson, James. "Rewriting *Dr. No* in 1962: James Bond and the End of the British Empire in Jamaica." *Small Axe* 19, no. 2 (2015): 56–76.

Rubin, Steven Jay. *The James Bond Films: A Behind the Scenes History*. London: Talisman Books, 1981.

——. *The James Bond Movie Encyclopedia*. Rev. ed. Chicago: Contemporary Books, 2003.

Sarris, Andrew, *The American Cinema: Directors and Directions 1929–1968*. New York: Da Capo Press, 1996 [1968].

Schenkman, Richard. "The Terence Young Interview." *Bondage* 10 (1981): 1–9.

Sedgwick, John. *Changing to Stay the Same: Hollywood, 1946 to 1965*. Discussion Papers in Business Economics 31. London: University of North London, 2001.

Sellers, Robert, *The Battle for Bond: The Genesis of Cinema's Greatest Hero*. Sheffield, UK: Tomahawk Press, 2007.

——. *When Harry Met Cubby: The Story of the James Bond Producers*. Stroud: The History Press, 2019.

Sitney, P. Adams. *Visionary Film: The American Avant-Garde, 1943–1978*. 2nd ed. Oxford: Oxford University Press, 1979.

Spicer, Andrew. *Sean Connery: Acting, Stardom, and National Identity*. Manchester: Manchester University Press, 2022.

Sutherland, John A. *Fiction and the Fiction Industry*. London: Athlone Press, 1978.

Thompson, Kristin, and David Bordwell. *Film History: An Introduction*. New York: McGraw-Hill, 1994.

Turner, Adrian. *Goldfinger*. Bloomsbury Movie Guide 2. London: Bloomsbury, 1998.

Usborne, Richard. *Clubland Heroes: A Nostalgic Study of Some Recurrent Characters in the Romantic Fiction of Dornford Yates, John Buchan, and Sapper*. London: Barrie & Jenkins, 1953.

Verhuel, Jaap, ed. *The Cultural Life of James Bond: Specters of 007*. Amsterdam: Amsterdam University Press, 2020.

Walker, Alexander, *Hollywood, England: The British Film Industry in the Sixties*. London: Michael Joseph, 1974.

Walker, Cynthia W. "*The Man from U.N.C.L.E.*: Ian Fleming's Other Spy." In *James Bond in World and Popular Culture: The Films Are Not Enough*, ed. Robert G. Weiner, B. Lynn Whitfield, and Jack Becker, 235–51. Newcastle, UK: Cambridge Scholars, 2010.

BIBLIOGRAPHY

Williams, Melanie. "Her Word Was Her Bond: Johanna Harwood, Bond's First Woman Screenwriter." In *From Blofeld to Moneypenny: Gender in James Bond*, ed. Steven Gerrard, 117–27. Bingley, UK: Emerald, 2020.

Wood, Linda, ed. *BFI Information Guide 1: British Film Industry*. London: British Film Institute Information and Education Department, 1980.

INDEX

ABC (American Broadcasting Company), 148
Action of the Tiger (1957), 61, 102
Adam, Ken, 57, 64, 70, 184; overcost on sets, 102–3, 109–10, 112; and set design, 127, 157–58
Adams, Alex, 31
African Queen, The (1951), 7
Alfie (1966), 82
Allen, Irving, 40, 42–45, 117
Allen, Patrick, 58
Altria, Bill, 7
Amis, Kingsley, 29, 31, 79–80
Andress, Ursula, 93, 100, 141, 169–70
Anna Karenina (BBC drama, 1961), 60
Another Time, Another Place (1958), 60
Anthony, Peter, 58
Armes, Roy, 4

Associated British Picture Corporation, 46
"Atticus," 87

Balio, Tino, 39, 61
Bandit of Zhobe, The (1959), 40
Barbarella (1968), 147
Barry, John, 110, 184
Barry Lyndon (1975), 157
Bay of Pigs invasion, 74
Beatles, The, 49, 52
Bergman, Ingrid, 9
Bergonzi, Bernard, 23
Betts, Ernest, 132–33
Big Country, The (1958), 6
Big Jim McLean (1952), 78
Billings, R. H. ("Josh"), 42, 134
Billy Liar (1963), 136
Binder, Maurice, 152–54
Bishop, George W., 16
Blaazer, Louis, 93

INDEX

Black Knight, The (1954), 40–41, 43
Blackwell, Blanche, 60, 96
Blackwell, Chris, 96
Blood Alley (1955), 78
Bloom, Claire, 60
Bonnie and Clyde (1967), 147
Booker, Christopher, 26
Boothroyd, Geoffrey, 21
Bordwell, David, 6
Braine, John, 46
Bridge on the River Kwai, The (1957), 7, 49
British Board of Film Censors, 82, 86
British Film Production Fund. *See* Eady levy
Broccoli, Albert R. ("Cubby"), 1, 4–5, 11, 39, 55, 56, 60, 63, 65, 78, 98, 117, 183; on Sean Connery, 168; criticism of US release of *Dr. No*, 140–41; partnership with Saltzman, 49–51; and Warwick Film Productions, 40–45
Bryanston Films, 47, 49, 52
Buccaneers, The (ITC series, 1956–1957), 59–60
Buchan, John, 16, 17, 90
Burton, Peter, 103
Burton, Richard, 46
Bustamante, Alexander, 94
Butler, R. A., 25
Buxton, David, 156, 166

Cabinet of Dr. Caligari, The (1920), 158
Call Me Bwana (1963), 114

Cameron, Ian, 133
Campaign for Nuclear Disarmament, 25
Cannadine, David, 19
Captain Gallant of the Foreign Legion (1956), 45
Captain Sindbad (1963), 143
Carter, Reggie, 92
Carver, Muriel, 114
Casablanca (1942), 9
Casino Royale (novel, 1953), 13–14, 18–19, 28, 31, 38, 48, 53, 79
Cawelti, John G., 32–33
CBS (Columbia Broadcasting System), 60
Chandler, Raymond, 16, 22–23
Charlie Chan in Panama (1940), 74
Chase, James Hadley, 24
Cheyney, Peter, 16
Churchill, Winston, 19, 24
Classics Illustrated, 141–42
Cleopatra (1963), 143
Cockleshell Heroes, The (1955), 40, 43, 69
Coe, Richard L., 140
Coleman, John, 129–30
Colman, Ronald, 167
Colour Box, A (1935), 155
Columbia Pictures, 40, 44, 49–50
Connery, Sean, 4, 8, 70, 96; casting as Bond, 60; critics' response to, 127–28; filming *Dr. No*, 84, 104–5; performance as Bond, 166–68, 184; US publicity of, 141
Corridor of Mirrors (1948), 184
Courtenay, Tom, 167

INDEX

Coward, Noël, 9
Craig, Michael, 58
Crowther, Bosley, 139–40
Croydon, John, 62–64
Cuban Missile Crisis, 135
Curse of Frankenstein, The (1957), 129

Dahl, Roald, 81
Daily Express, 14, 37, 58
Daily Gleaner, 58, 91–94, 148, 175–76
Dalton, Timothy, 2
Danger Man (ITC series, 1960–1964), 58
Danjaq SA, 40, 53–55, 112–14, 120
Darby O'Gill and the Little People (1959), 60
Darling (1965), 82
Davies, J. E. W. *See* Mather, Berkely
Dawson, Anthony, 100
Day the Earth Caught Fire, The (1961), 69
DC Comics, 142
Deadlier Than the Male (1967), 56
Deighton, Len, 17, 56
Denning, Michael, 27, 156, 170
Dent, Alan, 137
Diamonds Are Forever (novel, 1956), 14, 16, 18, 20–21, 53, 79
Dick Tracy's G-Men (1939), 74
Dixon of Dock Green (BBC series, 1955–1975), 175
Dodds, Klaus, 73–74
Dracula (1958), 129
Dr. Mabuse, the Gambler (1922), 158
Dr. No (film, 1962): box-office receipts of, 1, 120, 143–45, 147; budget of, 55–58; production of, 91–112; place of in film history, 1–8; promotion of, 140–42; reception in Britain, 125–38; reception in Jamaica, 147; reception in United States, 138–43; scripting of, 65–90
Dr. No (novel, 1958), 14, 19–36, 138, 162–63, 173
Dr. Strangelove; or, How I Learned to Stop Worrying and Love the Bomb (1964), 157
Duke, William, 100
Durgnat, Raymond, 174–75
Dyer, Peter John, 131–32

Eady levy, 41–42, 47, 55, 61
Eco, Umberto, 19, 160–63
Edward Dryhurst Productions, 48, 112
Ekberg, Anita, 114
Entertainer, The (1960), 45, 47, 62
Eon Productions, 39, 55, 61, 98–99, 119, 154
Eros Films, 44
Expresso Bongo (1959), 69

Felton, Norman, 55
Field, Matthew, 67
Film Finances, 10, 11, 48–49, 54, 124–25; completion guarantee for *Dr. No*, 61–64; monitoring production of *Dr. No*, 98–121
Finney, Albert, 167
Fire Down Below (1957), 40
Fisher, Terence, 129
Fleming, Ann (*née* Charteris), 13, 97–98

INDEX

Fleming, Ian, 1, 7–8, 11, 57, 70, 83, 87, 120, 183; and film rights, 54–55; and the James Bond books, 13–38; on location in Jamaica, 95–98; meeting Irving Allen, 44; and *The Man From U.N.C.L.E.*, 55; opinion of Sean Connery, 60
Flynn, Errol, 167
Follow That Man (1961), 116
Foot, Hugh, 34
For Your Eyes Only (short story collection, 1960), 14, 18, 53
Foster-Davis, William, 93, 175
Fox, James, 58
Frankenheimer, John, 5
Frightened City, The (1961), 60
From Russia with Love (film, 1963), 2, 60, 82, 117, 119, 144–45, 148, 178, 184
From Russia, with Love (novel, 1957), 14, 16, 20, 25, 48, 53, 138

Gable, Clark, 167
Gaitskell, Hugh, 25
Garrett, Robert, 49, 98–103, 106
Gayson, Eunice, 104–5, 169
Gill, Brandan, 140
Gilliat, Penelope, 129
Gilling, John, 42
Girl on the Boat, The (1961), 116
Godfrey, John, 13
Goldberg, Fred, 141
Goldfinger (film, 1964), 2, 6, 117, 120, 144–46, 148, 184
Goldfinger (novel, 1959), 14, 17, 53, 79, 138
Goldwyn Studios, 60

Grant, Cary, 58
Grant, Violet, 22
Grass Is Greener, The (1960), 152
Great Train Robbery, The (1903), 154
Green, Guy, 60
Gross, Larry, 185
Guinness, Alec, 56
Gunfight at the O.K. Corral (1957), 6
Guns of Navarone, The (1961), 7, 49, 135, 185

Hall, Sheldon, 10
Hamilton, Guy, 60
Hamilton, Richard, 155
Harbottle & Lewis, 48
Hard Day's Night, A (1964), 52
Harper, Sue, 168–69
Harris, Richard, 167
Harwood, Johanna, 57, 66–68, 83–87
Hawkins, Jack, 167
Hell Below Zero (1954), 40, 43, 69
Heller, Otto, 108
Hellions, The (1961), 45
Help! (1965), 52
Hepburn, Katharine, 45
Hibbin, Nina, 133
High Treason (1951), 78
Hill, Derek, 127
Hill, John, 171–72
Hines, Claire, 170
Hinxman, Margaret, 127
Hitchcock, Alfred, 5, 58, 128, 146, 172
Hoberman, J., 135
Hope, Bob, 45, 114
Hope, Peter, 114
Horak, Jan-Christopher, 154
Houston, Penelope, 88–89, 132
How the West Was Won (1962), 143

INDEX

Howard, Leslie, 167
Howard, Trevor, 58
Howard, Wren, 37
Hughes, Ken, 42, 60
Hunt, Peter, 184

I Could Go on Singing (1963), 116
Independent Television Programme Company, 59
Indiscreet (1958), 152
Interpol (1957), 40
Ipcress File, The (1965), 56, 108, 156
Iron Petticoat, The (1956), 45, 62, 99
I, Spy (NBC series, 1965–1968), 156
I, the Jury (1953), 134
ITV (Independent Television), 149
I Was a Communist for the FBI (1951), 78

Jack Paar Show, The (NBC late-night show, 1957–1962), 96
Jamaica Independence Act (1962), 95
James Bond Dossier, The (Amis), 29, 79
James Bond of the Secret Service, 38, 78
James Gunn—Secret Agent (unrealized film), 20
Jason and the Argonauts (1963), 143
Johnson, Paul, 23–24
Johnson, Richard, 58
Juarez (1938), 104
Juroe, Charles, 124

Karlson, Phil, 61
Kaufman, Stanley, 140
Keator, Dolores, 93

Kemsley Newspaper Group, 13
Kennedy, John F., 48, 74, 96
Kid for Two Farthings, A (novel), 69
Killers of Kilimanjaro (1959), 40
Kind of Loving, A (1962), 136
Kiss Me Deadly (1955), 134
Kitzmiller, John, 100, 177
Knight, Arthur, 140
Korda, Alexander, 52
Kravitz, Dick, 141
Krim, Arthur, 50, 123

Ladd, Alan, 41
Lang, Fritz, 131
Lancelot and Guinevere (1963), 115
Lane, Allen, 14
Larkin, Philip, 82
Lawrence of Arabia (1962), 7, 49, 143
le Carré, John, 17
LeWars, Marguerite, 92
Lee, Bernard, 103
Lee, Byron, 93, 176
Legion of Decency, 45, 147
Lewis, Brian, 48
Licence to Kill (1989), 70
Life (magazine), 48
Live and Let Die (film, 1973), 59
Live and Let Die (novel, 1954), 14, 19–20, 25, 34, 53, 79
Loneliness of the Long Distance Runner, The (1962), 136
Longest Day, The (1962), 143
Long Ships, The (1964), 45
Look Back in Anger (film, 1959), 45–46, 136
Look Back in Anger (play, 1956), 25
Lopert, Ilya, 124
Loren, Sophia, 69

INDEX

Love Is a Ball (1963), 116
Lucas, George, 6
Lycett, Andrew, 9, 48
Lye, Len, 155

McClory, Kevin, 38, 51, 54, 66, 78
McGilligan, Pat, 66
McGoohan, Patrick, 58–59
McQueen, Steve, 167
Magnificent Seven, The (1960), 6
Maibaum, Richard, 9, 43–44, 51, 57, 65–76, 80, 90
Manchurian Candidate, The (1962), 5
Man From U.N.C.L.E., The (NBC series, 1964–1968), 55
Man in a Suitcase (ITC series, 1967–1968), 156
Man with the Golden Gun, The (novel, 1965), 14, 19, 37, 79
Mankowitz, Wolf, 49, 57, 65–78, 80
Manley, Norman, 94
Marshall, Zena, 169
Mary Poppins (1964), 144
Mather, Berkely, 57, 66–67, 83–84
Mature, Victor, 41
Maxwell, Lois, 103
MGM (Metro-Goldwyn-Mayer), 61, 69
Miller, Count Prince, 93
Millionairess, The (1960), 69
Milne, Angela, 128–29
Modesty Blaise (1966), 156
Moonraker (film, 1979), 2
Moonraker (novel, 1955), 14, 16, 18, 20, 28, 38, 53
Moore, Roger, 58–59
Moore, Ted, 57, 100, 108, 160, 184
More, Kenneth, 167

Morgenthau, Henry, 20
Morton, Monty, 134
Mosley, Leonard, 88, 127
Motion Picture Export Association, 41
Mouse on the Moon, The (1963), 52, 116
Mouse That Roared, The (1959), 152
Moxon, Timothy, 93
Mr. Arkadin (1955), 83
Mulvey, Laura, 171–72
Mummy, The (1959), 129
Muni, Paul, 104

National Film Finance Corporation, 46
NBC (National Broadcasting Company), 55
Nehru, Jawaharlal, 178
Niven, David, 58
No Orchids for Miss Blandish (novel), 24
Norman, Monty, 93, 110, 184
North by Northwest (1959), 5, 6, 58
No Time to Die (1958), 40, 43, 61, 69

Octopussy and the Living Daylights (short story collection, 1966), 14
Olivier, Laurence, 46
On Her Majesty's Secret Service (film, 1969), 70
On Her Majesty's Secret Service (novel, 1963), 14, 96
Ornstein, George, 49, 59, 75, 119, 124
Orwell, George, 24
Osborne, John, 25, 45–46
Our Man Flint (1966), 147

INDEX

Paratrooper. See *Red Beret, The*
Pearson, John, 9, 95
Peeping Tom (1960), 108, 134
Penguin Books, 14
Penington, Jon, 114
Petrie, Duncan, 160
Picker, David, 51–53, 59–61, 75, 78, 118, 121, 124
Pinewood Studios, 7, 103–8
Pinter, Harold, 56
Planet of the Apes (1968), 6
Playboy (magazine), 170
Plomer, William, 20, 33
Porter, Edwin S., 154
Powell, Dilys, 128
Powell, Michael, 134
Preminger, Otto, 146
Prendergast, Lester, 93
Production Code Administration, 82, 146

Queen of Spades (1949), 108
Quennell, Peter, 48, 98
Quiller Memorandum, The (1966), 56

Raiders of the Lost Ark (1981), 6, 180
Rainbow Dance (1936), 155
Rank Film Distributors, 56
Rank Organization, 38
Ratoff, Gregory, 38, 53
Raven, Simon, 16
Red Beret, The (1953), 40–41, 43, 61, 69, 83, 102
Reed, Carol, 69
Reed, Clive, 100
Reisz, Karel, 47
Requiem for a Heavyweight (BBC drama, 1957), 60

Richard III (1955), 108
Richard, Cliff, 134
Richards, Dick, 127
Richardson, Tony, 45–46, 115
Rissik, Andrew, 167
Road to Hong Kong (1962), 152
Robertson, James, 95, 175–76
Robinson, David, 129
Room at the Top (1959), 26, 136
Rose, Tony, 132
"Rosie" (the tarantula), 108
Ross, Alan, 15–16
Rudkin, R. C., 57, 63

Safari (1956), 40, 43, 61, 102
Saltzman, Harry, 1, 10, 11, 67–68, 183; and partnership with Broccoli, 56–58; and producing *Dr. No*, 98–114; securing Bond option, 38, 48–49; told he "can only lose a million dollars," 123–25; and Woodfall Films, 45–51;
Saint, The (ITC series, 1962–1968), 59, 156
"Sapper," 17
Sapphire (1959), 178
Sarris, Andrew, 184
Saturday Night and Sunday Morning (1960), 45, 47, 62, 136
Schenkman, Richard, 67
Sedgwick, John, 145
Sellers, Peter, 69
Shaw, Robert, 59
Shot in the Dark, A (1964), 52
Silencers, The (1966), 147
Sillitoe, Alan, 47
Simmons, Bob, 58, 108

633 Squadron (1964), 52
Smith, Bernard, 106, 111–12
Sodom and Gomorrah (1962), 143
Sopel, Stanley, 57
Sound of Music, The (1965), 144
Spender, Stephen, 98
Spielberg, Steven, 6
Spillane, Mickey, 31, 134
Spy Who Loved Me, The (film, 1977), 2
Spy Who Loved Me, The (novel, 1962), 14, 162
Star Wars (1977), 6
Stead, Peter John, 22
Sternberg, Josef Von, 172
Suez Crisis, 19, 36
Sunday Times, 13, 87, 96
Sutherland, John, 14
Symons, Julian, 16

Tasca, Alessandro, 117
Tank Force. See *No Time to Die*
Taste of Honey, A (1961), 136
Thin Man, The (NBC series, 1957–1959), 69
This Sporting Life (1963), 136
Thomas, F. L., 56
Thompson, Kristin, 6
Thunderball (film, 1965), 2, 51, 66, 118, 121
Thunderball (novel, 1961), 14, 48, 51, 53–54, 78–79
Todd, Richard, 167
Tom Jones (1963), 52, 56, 82, 115–16, 118
Trials of Oscar Wilde, The (1960), 45, 157
True Lies (1994), 180

Tufnell, Satterthwaite & Co., 112
Tunes of Glory (1960), 56
Turner, Adrian, 70
Two Faces of Dr Jekyll (1960), 69
2001: A Space Odyssey (1968), 6
20,000 Leagues Under the Sea (1954), 92

United Artists, 1, 5, 7, 8, 11, 39, 61, 65, 75; distribution and financing agreements for Bond series, 53–55; and *Dr. No* overcost 113–21; initial response to *Dr. No*, 123–25, promotion of *Dr. No*. 96, 140–42; and receipts of Bond films, 144–45
Universal Pictures, 115

Valenti, Jack, 147
Valiant, The (1962), 52, 56, 59, 114, 116
View to a Kill, A (film, 1985), 59

Wait Until Dark (1967), 184
Walker, Alexander, 4, 46, 88, 124, 127
Walt Disney Company, 60, 92
Warhol, Andy, 155
Warner Bros., 46
Warwick Film Productions, 40–45, 55, 61, 69
Waugh, Evelyn, 97
Welles, Orson, 83, 185
Whitehall, Richard, 133–34
Whittingham, Jack, 51, 78
Widmark, Richard, 41
Wilcox, Herbert, 52
Wild Bunch, The (1969), 147
Wilde, Cornel, 115

INDEX

Wilder, Billy, 146
Williams, Melanie, 83
Wilson, Cecil, 128
Wiseman, Joseph, 57, 178
Wiseman, Thomas, 133
Woodfall Film Productions, 46–47, 52, 115
Woolf, James, 46
Woolf, John, 46

Young Ones, The, 134–35
Young, Terence, 5, 129, 135–36, 167–68; chosen to direct *Dr. No*, 61; contribution of to script, 67, 84; critical reputation of, 184–85; directing *Dr. No*, 99–105; Film Finances' opinion of, 61–64; payment of fee, 113, 120; with Warwick Films, 42, 57, 58;
You Only Live Twice (film, 1967), 2, 81
You Only Live Twice (novel, 1964), 14

Zarak (1956), 40, 43, 61, 70
Zec, Donald, 65
Zulu (1964), 7, 10, 185

GPSR Authorized Representative: Easy Access System Europe, Mustamäe tee
50, 10621 Tallinn, Estonia, gpsr.requests@easproject.com

www.ingramcontent.com/pod-product-compliance
Lightning Source LLC
Chambersburg PA
CBHW031240290426
44109CB00012B/379